The Lord of All Things
A Trilogy of Truth
Book Three

WALKING

IN

THE LIGHT

Following in His Steps

The Lord of All Things
A Trilogy of Truth
Book Three

WALKING IN THE LIGHT

Following in His Steps

JON VON ERNST

AVAILABLE AS AUDIOBOOK

thepureword.net

Copyright © 2023 By Jon von Ernst

The Lord of All Things Series - A Trilogy of Truth - Book Three

Walking in the Light
Following in His Steps

Printed in the United States of America
ISBN: 9798392568925

All rights reserved solely by the author. The author guarantees all contents are original and do not infringe upon the legal rights of any other person or work. No part of this book may be reproduced in any form without the permission of the author. The views expressed in this book are not necessarily those of the publisher.

All Scripture quotations are taken from the World English Bible, unless otherwise noted. The World English Bible is in the Public Domain, That means it is not copyrighted. However, "World English Bible" is a Trademark.

Scripture quotations marked (NASB) are taken from the New American Standard Bible®. Copyright © 1960, 1962, 1963, 1968, 1971, 1972, 1973, 1975, 1977, 1995 by The Lockman Foundation. Used by permission. (www.Lockman.org)

Scripture quotations marked (HCSB) are taken from the Holman Christian Standard Bible®, Copyright © 1999, 2000, 2002, 2003, 2009 by Holman Bible Publishers. Used by permission. Holman Christian Standard Bible®, Holman CSB®, and HCSB® are federally registered trademarks of Holman Bible Publishers.

Scripture quotations marked (NIV) are taken from the Holy Bible, New International Version, Copyright © 1973, 1978, 1984 by Int'l Bible Society.

Scripture quotations marked (KJV) are taken from The King James Version of the Holy Bible, public domain.

Scripture quotations marked (TFLV) are taken from The Father's Life Version, 3rd edition, 2016, by A Grain of Wheat Ministries.

Scripture quotations marked (DRA) are taken from Douay-Rheims 1899 American Edition, public domain.

Correspondence may be addressed to the author at: thepureword@yahoo.com

www.thepureword.net - Books by Jon von Ernst

Dedication

The LORD is my light and my salvation;
whom shall I fear?
The LORD is the strength of my life;
of whom shall I be afraid?

For with thee is the fountain of life:
in thy light shall we see light.
O continue thy lovingkindness unto them that know thee;
and thy righteousness to the upright in heart.

O send out thy light and thy truth:
let them lead me;
let them bring me unto thy holy hill,
and to thy tabernacles.

Thy word is a lamp unto my feet,
and a light unto my path.

The entrance of thy words giveth light;
it giveth understanding unto the simple.

Psalm 27:1, 36:9-10, 43:3, 119:105, 130

Table of Contents

Dedication .... *v*
Preface .... *vii*
Introduction .... *x*

A Righteous God 1
Knowing the Truth 8
No Condemnation 20
Set Free to Walk by the Spirit 31
A Wretched Man 43
Escaping the Devil's Trap 54
That He Might Have Mercy 66
On All 66
Grace 76
No Respecter of Persons 88
Unmerited Favor 96
Eternal Security 108
No One Can Take Us 116
Out of His Hand 116
He Will Never Forsake Us 125
Take Heed Lest You Fall 134
Worthy of the Kingdom 144
An Intimate Relationship 156
Following in His Steps 167
Epilogue 182

Preface

This book, *Walking in the Light – Following in His Steps,* is the third book in the series "The Lord of All Things – A Trilogy of Truth." It takes the reader even deeper into the truths of scripture. It reveals truths hidden within some of the more misunderstood passages of scripture and demonstrates the danger that comes from misunderstanding these passages.

It deals with often misunderstood subjects, such as the believer's view of sin in the church and in the world. It considers the proper understanding of Romans, chapters five through eight and the impact that our understanding of those chapters has on how we live our Christian lives.

This book examines the meanings of the words, mercy and grace, and the effect our understanding of those words has on our walk as Christians. It also takes an extended look into the question of eternal security as presented in the scriptures. Finally, and perhaps most importantly, this book examines how Christ walked while on this earth and what implications His walk has on what God expects of us.

Book One, *The Gospel of the Kingdom – God's Eternal Purpose in Christ,* reveals God's plan of love and mercy to redeem every person in the world back to Himself. It reveals how any person, no matter who they are, where they are from, or what they have done, can receive this gift of God's mercy. It also reveals how those that choose to receive this gift become a new creation, reconciled to God, having all their past sins forgiven.

This book includes a basic primer on living the Christian life, both individually and as a member of the body of Christ, the church. It also reveals scriptural truths concerning life after death and the coming judgment.

Book Two, *The Victorious Christian – Inheriting the Promises,* takes the reader a little deeper into the truths of the scriptures. It reveals God's provision to equip every true believer to overcome every obstacle and endure to the end, inheriting all the promises of God. This book focuses on the essential role that the Holy Spirit, dwelling within the believer, has in the Christian life.

It encourages the believer to grow in faith and in the knowledge of our Lord Jesus Christ as they walk by the Spirit. It reveals how a steadfast walk by faith will prepare them for our Lord's soon return.

Every chapter of these books focuses on at least one specific truth as presented in the scriptures concerning Jesus Christ our Lord and our lives as His followers. Some chapters also focus on exposing some of the more popular false teachings common in many churches today. To combat these false teachings, we proclaim Christ, the living Word of God. When we do, the light of His life will expose these false teachings as lies.

Therefore, my goal in this book is simply to proclaim Christ, and the truth as it is in Christ. My desire is to let the light of the Word shine through the words of this book. As you read through these books, you may experience the light of God's word shining on you and revealing things in your life that are displeasing to God.

If you are uncomfortable with having the light of the Word shine upon you, upon your beliefs, and upon how you are living your life, perhaps you will not want to read any further. However, if you desire a fresh start in your life, if you desire a closer walk, a closer relationship with God, and are willing to be made a little uncomfortable, you may want to continue reading. If something is exposed in what you believe or in how you are living that is not pleasing to God, perhaps your desire for the truth will lead you to repent, turning back to God and drawing closer to Him.

It is not my intention to offend anyone, but to speak the truth as it is in Christ and to allow the light of the Word to shine through. My prayer is that the Word would draw the unbeliever to Jesus, and bring every genuine believer into a more intimate relationship with our Father in heaven, that we all might walk as Jesus walked, that we might follow in His steps!

These book presents these truths in practical applications for our individual Christian lives and for our corporate church life. These truths are presented to encourage believers to walk in faithful obedience to the leading of the Holy Spirit, believing the truth as set forth in the scriptures.

God is glorified as we demonstrate our love for Him through our obedience and through our love for one another. We do this by speaking the truth to one another and encouraging each other to gladly suffer for Christ and to endure faithfully to the end.

These books have been designed as a resource for Bible study for both individuals and groups. The questions at the end of each chapter are intended to stimulate thought and discussion concerning the truths covered in each chapter and how they apply to our lives.

It is my hope that these books will help each reader and each listener come to a deeper understanding of our God and of His ways. I pray that every person that reads or listens to these books will come to know Jesus as "*The Lord of All Things*" in their own lives.

Jon von Ernst

Introduction

It is important that the reader understand the danger of accepting the teachings of this author, or any other author, pastor, or teacher at face value. No person's teachings should be blindly accepted. When we, without question, accept anyone's teachings, we place ourselves in danger of being led astray. There are many false teachers in the world and in the church today. It is essential that we try the spirits and that we take any teaching, no matter how famous or highly revered the teacher may be, to the Scriptures for verification. This author encourages you to take the teachings of this book to the Scriptures and search them out diligently.

When we take teachings to the Scriptures, it is important to look up and review the context of the passages that the teacher has referred to. It may be even more important to allow the Spirit to direct us to passages that appear to contradict the conclusions presented by the teacher. Usually there is more than one perspective presented in Scripture for any individual truth. This is due to the incredible depth of the manifold wisdom of God. It is the tendency of natural man to see, at most, only one side of any truth presented in Scripture. It is therefore necessary for the reader, the listener, to look to the Holy Spirit to reveal more than just one aspect of any truth in question. We should desire God to reveal to us as many aspects of the specific truth as He is willing to show us, and that we are able and prepared to receive.

Our initial desire in searching out in the Scriptures the truths that are being taught is to verify if the teachings do in fact have a scriptural basis and are properly applied. Our secondary goal is to broaden our understanding of the specific truth being taught by seeing that truth from other perspectives, thereby deepening our understanding of our God and of His ways. As we come to see various aspects of any truth, we will become more accepting of other believers, and of their individual understanding of the truths that they have come to believe and embrace. This will enable us to more effectively maintain the unity of the Spirit and reduce the tendency to separate ourselves from other believers simply because we have stumbled upon some teaching about which there are different understandings.

It is important for all of us to realize that none of us has all understanding or all knowledge of the truths presented in Scripture. At best, we see in part, and we understand in part. We are all disciples. We are all students. We are all in the process of learning. The only way any of us can learn is if we begin by humbling ourselves and admit that we do not have all the answers. We need to consider others as better than ourselves and realize that if we have an ear to hear, God can teach us by His Spirit through the speaking of any brother or sister. When we think too highly of ourselves, we have greatly reduced our ability to learn.

Our ultimate goal, in coming to the Scriptures, is to be fed. We must come to the Scriptures as those that are hungry for the living word of God, Jesus Christ our Lord. Our desire should be to know Him. May God give us the grace and the hunger to hear God's speaking by His Spirit through the Scriptures and through every brother or sister that we fellowship with. Perhaps if we are hungry enough, God will feed us with more of Christ, that at His return, we may know Him and be found in Him!

May we be those that are truly taught by the Holy Spirit and not by men.

Jon von Ernst

Chapter 1

A Righteous God

I have had the privilege of fellowshipping with believers in various parts of the country, in several different denominations, and in various settings. Sometimes the fellowship would be in group Bible studies, and sometimes with just one or two brothers sharing with one another the things that have been on our hearts.

Inevitably, concerns would be shared about the disturbing amount of sin in our country and throughout the world. There would be special concern about the seemingly rapid increase in the level of sin, the level of evil taking place around us. It seems that, almost on a daily basis, we are confronted with more and more examples of the growing degradation of society.

Eventually, the discussion often turned to Paul's detailed account in Romans chapter one of God's judgment on people that had exchanged the truth of God for a lie. We would be reminded of how God delivered such people over to a worthless or reprobate mind to do what is morally wrong. According to Paul, these people were filled with all unrighteousness, evil, greed, and wickedness.

He explains their situation saying, "For God's wrath is revealed from heaven against all godlessness and unrighteousness of people who by their unrighteousness suppress the truth, since what can be known about God is evident among them, because God has shown it to them. For His invisible attributes, that is, His eternal power and divine nature, have been clearly seen since the creation of the world, being understood through what He has made. As a result, people are without excuse.

"And because they did not think it worthwhile to acknowledge God, God delivered them over to a worthless mind to do what is morally wrong. They are filled with all unrighteousness, evil, greed, and wickedness. They are full of envy, murder, quarrels, deceit, and malice. They are gossips, slanderers, God-haters arrogant, proud, boastful, inventors of evil, disobedient, to parents, undiscerning, untrustworthy, unloving, and unmerciful. Although they know full well God's just sentence—that those who practice such things deserve to die—they not only do them, but even applaud others who practice them." (Romans 1:18-20, 28-32, HCSB).

This passage seemed to describe so clearly what we saw playing out right in front of our eyes. It seemed to give us an assurance of the righteousness of God. He had given them every opportunity to know God and acknowledge Him as God. Yet knowing God, they refused to glorify Him as God. Claiming to be wise, they became fools and exchanged the glory of the immortal God for images resembling mortal man, birds, four-footed animals, and reptiles. As a result, people are without excuse.

Therefore, God delivered them over to the cravings of their evil hearts. He gave them over to a worthless reprobate mind to do what is morally wrong.

Although they know full well God's just sentence, that those who practice such things deserve to die, they not only do them, but even rejoice when others practice them. However, "God is righteous and will repay each one according to his works" (Romans 2:6).

These considerations are often followed by a discussion of how we are eagerly awaiting the Lord's return. We look forward to Jesus coming to rule on the earth with a rod of iron. We rejoice that He will have Satan bound for 1,000 years as we rule and reign with Him after He has finally restored righteousness to the earth.

Walking in the Light

However, God has recently been opening the eyes of my understanding, little by little, revealing things in the Bible that I had read many times before yet did not understand. One such incident occurred this morning as I was reading this passage in Romans chapter one.

As I continued reading on into chapter two, I was shocked to realize who Paul, through the Holy Spirit's guidance, was writing to. He writes, "Therefore, any one of you who judges is without excuse. For when you judge another, you condemn yourself, since you, the judge, do the same things" (Romans 2:1, HCSB).

When Paul says, "Any one of you," who is he referring to? Any one of who? The answer to this question can be found in chapter one, verse seven, "To all that be in Rome, beloved of God, called to be saints: Grace to you and peace from God our Father, and the Lord Jesus Christ" (KJV).

Paul is addressing this passage in Romans 2 to the believers, the church in Rome. He writes, "Therefore, any one of you who judges is without excuse. For when you judge another, you condemn yourself, since you, the judge, do the same things. We know that God's judgment on those who do such things is based on the truth. Do you really think—anyone of you who judges those who do such things yet do the same—that you will escape God's judgment? Or do you despise the riches of His kindness, restraint, and patience, not recognizing that God's kindness is intended to lead you to repentance?

"But because of your hardness and unrepentant heart you are storing up wrath for yourself in the day of wrath, when God's righteous judgment is revealed. He will repay each one according to his works: eternal life to those who by persistence in doing good seek glory, honor, and immortality; but wrath and indignation to those who are self-seeking and disobey the truth but are obeying unrighteousness; affliction and distress for every human being who does evil, first to the Jew, and also to the Greek; but glory, honor, and peace for everyone who does what is good, first to the Jew, and also to the

Greek. There is no favoritism with God" (Romans 2:1-11, HCSB).

Here Paul is addressing the problem in the church of how believers see the sinners in the world living in the wretchedness of their sins and they judge them, even though they themselves, the believers, do the same things that they judge. In the church, we are often quick to judge the sinfulness of those in the world while we wink at the sin in the church, the sins being committed by the professing Christians.

Paul's point in this passage is that there is no favoritism with God. He is not a respecter of people. Whether you are a believer or a nonbeliever, He will judge each one righteously. Remember, "God is righteous and will repay each one according to his works." God will judge the world, but first God will judge the church. God's judgment begins with the house of God.

Peter explains, "For the time has come for judgment to begin with God's household, and if it begins with us, what will the outcome be for those who disobey the gospel of God?" (1 Peter 4:17, HCSB). God is a righteous God. He will judge His people. He is even more concerned about judging us than He is about judging the world.

How is God going to judge the church? What will He use to judge His people?

Peter addresses these questions saying, "If anyone suffers as a 'Christian,' he should not be ashamed but should glorify God in having that name. For the time has come for judgment to begin with God's household, and if it begins with us, what will the outcome be for those who disobey the gospel of God?

"And if a righteous person is saved with difficulty, what will become of the ungodly and the sinner? So those who suffer according to God's will should, while doing what is good, entrust themselves to a faithful Creator" (1 Peter 4:16-19).

Those of you who are parents, how is it with you? Are you more concerned with disciplining your own child or your neighbor's child. In the same way, God is more concerned with disciplining His own children, those that own Him as their Father. This discipline is a clear demonstration of the Father's love.

In His righteousness, God judges His people. He disciplines His people. He disciplines us because He loves us. He wants us, His people, to be holy because He is holy. He uses discipline to teach us, to purge and purify us, to cleanse us from all unrighteousness. We must accept His discipline, submit to His authority, repenting and turning back to Him, that we might be trained by it.

The writer of Hebrews illustrates this saying, "My son, do not take the Lord's discipline lightly or faint when you are reproved by Him, for the Lord disciplines the one He loves and punishes every son He receives.

"Endure suffering as discipline: God is dealing with you as sons. For what son is there that a father does not discipline? But if you are without discipline—which all receive—then you are illegitimate children and not sons. Furthermore, we had natural fathers discipline us, and we respected them.

"Shouldn't we submit even more to the Father of spirits and live? For they disciplined us for a short time based on what seemed good to them, but He does it for our benefit, so that we can share His holiness. No discipline seems enjoyable at the time, but painful. Later on, however, it yields the fruit of peace and righteousness to those who have been trained by it" (Hebrews 12:5-11, HCSB).

We have a choice. We, as believers, can choose to submit to the discipline of the Lord now and later reap the fruit of peace and righteousness, or we can reject His discipline, storing up for ourselves wrath in the day of wrath, and be judged by Him at the judgment seat of God.

Paul reminds the Christians in the church at Rome, "We shall all stand before the judgment seat of Christ. For it is written, 'As I live, saith the Lord, every knee shall bow to me, and every tongue shall confess to God.' So then every one of us shall give account of himself to God" (Romans 14:10-12, HCSB).

God will judge Christians for how they live. Remember Paul's words, "Do you really think—anyone of you who judges those who do such things yet do the same—that you will escape God's judgment? Or do you despise the riches of His kindness, restraint, and patience, not recognizing that God's kindness is intended to lead you to repentance?" (Romans 2:3-4, HCSB).

Again, to illustrate God's desire to lead us to repentance, Paul writes, "Even if I caused you sorrow by my letter, I do not regret it. Though I did regret it—I see that my letter hurt you, but only for a little while— yet now I am happy, not because you were made sorry, but because your sorrow led you to repentance. For you became sorrowful as God intended and so were not harmed in any way by us.

"Godly sorrow brings repentance that leads to salvation and leaves no regret, but worldly sorrow brings death. See what this godly sorrow has produced in you: what earnestness, what eagerness to clear yourselves, what indignation, what alarm, what longing, what concern, what readiness to see justice done.

"At every point you have proved yourselves to be innocent in this matter. So even though I wrote to you, it was neither on account of the one who did the wrong nor on account of the injured party, but rather that before God you could see for yourselves how devoted to us you are. By all this we are encouraged" (2 Corinthians 7:8-13, NIV).

Writing to the believers in the church in Corinth, Paul reminds them, "Therefore we also have as our ambition, whether at home or absent, to be pleasing to Him. For we must all appear before the judgment seat of Christ, so that each one may receive compensation for his deeds done through the body, in accordance with what he has done, whether good or bad. Therefore, knowing the fear of the Lord, we persuade people" (2 Corinthians 5:9-11, NASB).

Our God is a righteous God. He will judge sin, whether it is among the unbelieving people of this world, or among the believers in the church, the house of God. He is no respecter of persons. He does not show favoritism! He is righteous and He is just.

Chapter 1 Discussion Questions:
A Righteous God

1. Why did God give the people over to a worthless reprobate mind?
2. What is God's just sentence against those that practice unrighteousness?
3. When will Jesus rule the earth with a rod of iron?
4. Who was Paul referring to when he said, "Any one of you who judges is without excuse"?
5. Who do we condemn when we judge another yet do the same things?
6. What is God's kindness intended to accomplish?
7. What are we storing up for ourselves because of our hardness and unrepentant heart?
8. Where does God's judgment begin?
9. Who is God most concerned about judging?
10. What is a clear demonstration of the Father's love?
11. What does discipline produce in those who have been trained by it?
12. What will God's judgment of Christians be based on?

Chapter 2

Knowing the Truth

God expects His people to live holy lives, now, in this sinful world. To remind us of this, Peter writes, "Just as he who called you is holy, you yourselves also be holy in all of your behavior; because it is written, 'You shall be holy; for I am holy'" (1 Peter 1:15-16).

God's expectation is a just expectation, because He has given His people everything required to live holy lives. Again Peter writes, "His divine power has given us everything we need for a godly life through our knowledge of Him who called us by His own glory and goodness" (2 Peter 1:3, NIV).

God has given His people everything they need to walk as Jesus walked. John tells us, "This is how we know we are in Him: Whoever claims to live in Him must live as Jesus did" (1 John 2:5-6, NIV).

Many churches are filled with sinful behavior. Surveys have shown that there is virtually no difference between the church and the world when it comes to sinful living. One of the most grievous sins being tolerated in the church today is the teaching of false doctrine departing from the faith, even denying the Master who bought us. There are many in the church today teaching destructive heresies, undermining the faith of many.

Jude writes warning the believers, "Dear friends, although I was eager to write you about the salvation we share, I found it necessary to write and exhort you to contend for the faith that was delivered to the saints once for all. For some men, who were designated for this judgment long ago, have

Walking in the Light

come in by stealth; they are ungodly, turning the grace of our God into promiscuity and denying Jesus Christ, our only Master and Lord . . . These people are discontented grumblers, walking according to their desires; their mouths utter arrogant words, flattering people for their own advantage" (Jude 3-4, 16)

Peter also warns us describing the false teachers that will come among us, "But there were also false prophets among the people, just as there will be false teachers among you. They will secretly bring in destructive heresies, even denying the Master who bought them, and will bring swift destruction on themselves. Many will follow their unrestrained ways, and the way of truth will be blasphemed because of them. They will exploit you in their greed with deceptive words. Their condemnation, pronounced long ago, is not idle, and their destruction does not sleep" (2 Peter 2:1-3).

Paul challenges believers to consider the situation within the church, "Do you really think—anyone of you who judges those who do such things yet do the same—that you will escape God's judgment? Or do you despise the riches of His kindness, restraint, and patience, not recognizing that God's kindness is intended to lead you to repentance?"

Ignoring passages such as this, these false teachers preach, "Peace, peace." when there is no peace. They claim that Christians will not be judged for sin, because all our sins, past present, and future, were all forgiven at the time we were saved. They assure them that when God looks at us, He doesn't see our sinful living, He sees Jesus!

This concept reminds me of a song popular in Christian circles. "I am covered over with the robe of righteousness that Jesus gives to me . . When He looks at me, He sees not what I used to be, but He sees Jesus."

Those that falsely teach that God doesn't see our sinful living forget that the song is speaking of one that has repented, confessed his sins, and has had the blood of Christ applied to not just cover up his sins, but to take them away. It speaks of one that has turned away from his sinful past, what he used to be, and has turned to God, continually trusting Christ to empower him to live a holy life, pleasing to God.

If God looks at us and sees Jesus, it is only because we are actually living just as Jesus lived, in total obedience to the Father. The Apostle John reminds us of God's expectation for every believer, "But if anyone obeys His word, love for God is truly made complete in them. This is how we know we are in Him: Whoever claims to live in Him must live as Jesus did" (1 John 2:5-6, NIV).

The righteousness that we receive by faith in Jesus does not blind God to how we are living. It does not blind God to our real character. He sees us as we really are. In fact, the scriptures say that we stand before Him naked. Hebrews 4:13 reminds us, "There is no creature that is hidden from his sight, but all things are naked and laid open before the eyes of him to whom we must give an account."

Some teach that you don't need to know Jesus as Lord. They despise the idea of being a slave and Jesus being their Master. Jude warns believers, "For certain people have crept in unnoticed . . . ungodly persons who turn the grace of our God into indecent behavior and deny our only Master and Lord, Jesus Christ" (Jude 4).

They claim you can simply receive Jesus as your savior, and your sins will all be forgiven, and when you die, you will go to heaven to be with the Lord forever. There is, they say, no obligation to obey Him. His commands are only suggestions. Therefore, there is no Lordship, no judgment, no accountability.

Peter warns the believers, "There will be false teachers among you. They will secretly introduce destructive heresies, even denying the sovereign Lord who bought them—bringing swift destruction on themselves" (2 Peter 2:1). Paul also warns us, "Now the Spirit explicitly says that in later times some will depart from the faith, paying attention to deceitful spirits and the teachings of demons, through the hypocrisy of liars whose consciences are seared" (1 Timothy 4:1-2).

Walking in the Light

As Peter, Paul, and Jude prophesied, these false teachers are brazenly operating in the church today. Some teach that the believer needs to be under the law, needs to obey all of the statutes, commandments, and ordinances set forth in the Jewish religion.

The result is that those that believe this false teaching end up enslaved again to the law. If they fail in just one point, they are guilty of breaking the whole law. James writes to us setting forth this truth, "For whoever keeps the entire law, yet fails in one point, is guilty of breaking it all" (James 2:10).

Others teach that we are justified by grace through faith, and not of works. They claim that if we do any works to please God, we have fallen from grace. They claim that all our sins, past, present, and future are forgiven when we first believe. Therefore, they are not concerned in the least about sin. Some claim that they never even have to repent of any sin after they first believe.

They do not realize that whoever sins becomes a slave of sin. They do not realize that every sin is serious in God's eyes and must be repented of and turned from immediately. This is Paul's warning to the believers from Romans 6:16. "Don't you know that if you offer yourselves to someone as obedient slaves, you are slaves of that one you obey—either of sin leading to death or of obedience leading to righteousness?" (HCSB).

Remember how Paul had earlier warned the believers in the second chapter of Romans, "But because of your hardness and unrepentant heart you are storing up wrath for yourself in the day of wrath, when God's righteous judgment is revealed. He will repay each one according to his works: eternal life to those who by persistence in doing good seek glory, honor, and immortality; but wrath and indignation to those who are self-seeking and disobey the truth but are obeying unrighteousness, affliction and distress for every human being who does evil, first to the Jew, and also to the Greek; but glory, honor, and peace for everyone who does what is good, first to the Jew, and also to the Greek. There is no favoritism with God" (Romans 2:5-11).

Again, Paul warns the believers in the churches of Galatia, "Don't be deceived: God is not mocked. For whatever a man sows he will also reap, because the one who sows to his flesh will reap corruption from the flesh, but the one who sows to the Spirit will reap eternal life from the Spirit. So we must not get tired of doing good, for we will reap at the proper time if we don't give up. Therefore, as we have opportunity, we must work for the good of all, especially for those who belong to the household of faith" Galatians 6:7-10).

There are several reasons why these false teachings have gone virtually unchallenged in most churches. One of the main reasons is that so many within the churches do not know the truth, they do not know Jesus. Many have never even received the Holy Spirit. They have not been born again. Consequently, many professing Christians are virtually ignorant of the scriptures.

Jesus told the religious leaders of His day, "You are deceived, because you don't know the Scriptures or the power of God" (Matthew 22:29, HCSB). Because they do not know the truth, they are unable to detect false teachings when they hear them. Devoid of the Spirit, they also lack the boldness to challenge false doctrine when they hear it.

The secret to being delivered from the deception of these false teachings is to know the scriptures and the power of God, the power of the Holy Spirit dwelling within the born-again believer. The secret is to know the truth, to know Christ.

We must meet Jesus. We must have a genuine, living relationship with Him wherein we come to know Him as both Lord and Christ. It is not enough to know about Jesus. We must know Him personally. We must live in a close intimate relationship with Him as our Lord and Master.

We must have the same revelation that Peter had in Matthew 16:16 when Jesus asked him who he thought Jesus was. Peter said, "Thou art the Christ, the Son of the living God." In the next verse, Jesus responded to Peter saying,

"Blessed art thou, Simon Barjona: for flesh and blood hath not revealed it unto thee, but my Father which is in heaven." Have you ever had a revelation of who this Jesus is?

This Jesus is the Christ that died on the cross in our place that our sins might be forgiven. But, much more than this, He died on the cross that we would be delivered, set free, that we would no longer be slaves of sin. By His death and resurrection, Christ set us free from the penalty of sin, but much more, He set us free, liberated us, from the power of sin in our flesh. Now the sin in our flesh cannot force us to sin. Now the believer must choose to sin, being drawn away and enticed by his own evil desires.

James explains, "Let no man say when he is tempted, 'I am tempted by God,' for God can't be tempted by evil, and he himself tempts no one. But each one is tempted when he is drawn away by his own lust and enticed. Then the lust, when it has conceived, bears sin. The sin, when it is full grown, produces death" (James 1:13-15).

Paul reminds us in Romans 6:3-4, "Are you unaware that all of us who were baptized into Christ Jesus were baptized into His death? Therefore we were buried with Him by baptism into death, in order that, just as Christ was raised from the dead by the glory of the Father, so we too may walk in a new way of life." Through the baptism of the Holy Spirit, we died with Christ. This was necessary so that we also, like Christ, could walk in newness of life.

Through the power of Christ's death and resurrection, genuine believers have been liberated, freed from being slaves of sin and of the law. "For if we have been joined with Him in the likeness of His death, we will certainly also be in the likeness of His resurrection. For we know that our old self was crucified with Him in order that sin's dominion over the body may be abolished, so that we may no longer be enslaved to sin, since a person who has died is freed from sin's claims. . . So, you too consider yourselves dead to sin but alive to God in Christ Jesus" (Romans 6:5-6,11).

We have been made alive to God in Christ Jesus to glorify Him. We glorify Him by obeying Him.

Jesus warns us, "Not everyone who says to Me, 'Lord, Lord!' will enter the kingdom of heaven, but only the one who does the will of My Father in heaven. On that day many will say to Me, 'Lord, Lord, didn't we prophesy in Your name, drive out demons in Your name, and do many miracles in Your name?' Then I will announce to them, 'I never knew you! Depart from Me, you lawbreakers!'" (Matthew 7:21-23).

It does not matter what great thing we may do for God. If it is not out of obedience it is lawlessness. Obedience is better than sacrifice (1 Samuel 15:22). Paul reminds us, "If I donate all my goods to feed the poor, and if I give my body to be burned, but do not have love, I gain nothing" (1 Corinthians 13:3).

Again, Jesus warns us, "Therefore, everyone who hears these words of Mine and acts on them will be like a sensible man who built his house on the rock. . . But everyone who hears these words of Mine and doesn't act on them will be like a foolish man who built his house on the sand. The rain came down, the floods came, and the winds blew and beat on that house; and it fell—and its fall was great." (Matthew 7:24,26-27).

This is why it is so important that we also know Jesus as Lord. We must know Him as the supreme authority in our lives. It is not enough to know that He is Lord, we need to know Him as our Lord. We must listen to His speaking to us, but we also must submit to Him as Lord in all obedience, acting according to all that He instructs us to do.

In order to understand what it means for Jesus to be our Lord, we must understand the process of redemption. To redeem something means to purchase it back. If you owned something, and somehow lost ownership of it, it is necessary for you to pay a price to purchase it again. This is what Jesus did for us.

Through Adam's sin, mankind fell under Satan's power. Jesus paid the price, offering up His life to purchase us back to God. We, through sin, had become enslaved to sin and thereby enslaved to Satan. We were slaves of the one we obeyed.

Jesus, however, voluntarily gave His life for us to purchase us back to Himself. We now belong to Him. He owns us! We are His slaves, and He is our Lord. The ironic thing is that when we were slaves of sin, we had no freedom. Now, as slaves of God and of Christ, we are free. We are free to walk in obedience to our Lord! We are free to enjoy life in abundance.

Paul exhorts us, "Don't you know that your body is a sanctuary of the Holy Spirit who is in you, whom you have from God? You are not your own, for you were bought at a price. Therefore glorify God in your body" (1 Corinthians 6:19-20).

Paul's exhortation continues, "For he who is called by the Lord as a slave is the Lord's freedman. Likewise he who is called as a free man is Christ's slave. You were bought at a price; do not become slaves of men" (1 Corinthians 7:22-23).

Our very simple responsibility, as slaves, is to listen to our Lord and Master, Jesus, and follow Him, obeying Him. Hearing His voice requires a closeness to Him, an intimacy with Him. Jesus declares, "My sheep hear My voice, I know them, and they follow Me" (John 10:27).

Remember, "God is righteous and will repay each one according to his works" (Romans 2:6). There is no favoritism with God. He is not a respecter of people. He will judge the unrighteous, whether they profess to believe in Christ or not. The judgment of those that knew Jesus as their Lord and Savior will be much worse, much more severe, because they had been given so much.

Again, Jesus instructs us saying, "The one who did not know and did things deserving of blows will be beaten lightly. Much will be required of everyone who has been given much. And even more will be expected of the one who has been entrusted with more" (Luke 12:48).

Speaking of these false teachers, Peter warns, "They promise them freedom, but they themselves are slaves of corruption, since people are enslaved to whatever defeats them. For if, having escaped the world's impurity through the knowledge of our Lord and Savior Jesus Christ, they are again entangled in these things and defeated, the last state is worse for them than the first. For it would have been better for them not to have known the way of righteousness than, after knowing it, to turn back from the holy command delivered to them" (2 Peter 2:19-21).

In 2 Timothy chapter two, Paul is describing false teachers whose words spread like gangrene. He says they have deviated from the truth, teaching lies and overturning the faith of some. Nevertheless, God is merciful and compassionate to those who humble themselves and repent, turning away from unrighteousness and turning back to the Lord.

Paul writes, "The Lord knows those who are His, and Everyone who names the name of the Lord must turn away from unrighteousness. Now in a large house there are not only gold and silver bowls, but also those of wood and clay, some for honorable use, some for dishonorable. So if anyone purifies himself from these things, he will be a special instrument, set apart, useful to the Master, prepared for every good work" (2 Timothy 2:19-21).

If anyone purifies himself from these things, the false teachings, he will be a special instrument, set apart, useful to the Master and prepared for every good work. When we read the scriptures, whenever we go before the Lord in prayer, we must humble ourselves. We must prepare our hearts to receive correction and instruction from the Lord. We must allow the Lord to search us and reveal anything within us that is not pleasing to Him.

In this way we will be able to purge ourselves, through the leading and empowering of His indwelling Holy Spirit, of any false teachings that we have embraced and possibly even taught to others. As He exposes each one of these false teachings or incorrect understandings of scripture, in all

Walking in the Light

humility, we must repent, letting go of them, and laying hold of the truth as it is in Christ Jesus. We will then be encouraged by the Lord's Spirit to speak truth to one another in love. In this way, God will be glorified and the church, the body of Christ, the bride, will be prepared for the return of our Lord and Savior Jesus the Christ!

We are in a spiritual battle. We are in a spiritual warfare over the souls of men. Our enemy is using every tactic at his disposal. God has been aware, from the beginning, of this spiritual war and Satan's plan to dethrone God and destroy God's people. Therefore, God has provided us with everything we need to withstand the enemies attack, and yes, to be victorious over him through the victory of Jesus Christ our Lord.

Through the baptism of the Holy Spirit, God has given to every genuine Christian everything required for life and godliness. In the Spirit of Truth that He has given to indwell us, He has given us everything needed to withstand these false teachings and other attacks of the Devil.

God placed the Spirit of Christ, the Spirit of Truth, within each true believer to enable us to discern false teaching when we hear it. This indwelling Spirit not only teaches us the truth as it is in Christ Jesus, He also strengthens us by the vast strength of His indestructible life to confront the false teachers. He empowers us to put on the whole armor of God so that we might stand against the tactics of the Devil.

Paul exhorts us, "Let no one deceive you with empty words. For because of these things, the wrath of God comes on the children of disobedience. Therefore don't be partakers with them. For you were once darkness, but are now light in the Lord. Walk as children of light, for the fruit of the Spirit is in all goodness and righteousness and truth, proving what is well pleasing to the Lord. Have no fellowship with the unfruitful deeds of darkness, but rather even reprove them" (Ephesians 5:6-11).

Again, Paul writes exhorting us, "Finally, be strong in the Lord, and in the strength of his might. Put on the whole armor of God, that you may be able to stand against the wiles of the devil. For our wrestling is not against flesh and blood, but against the principalities, against the powers, against the world's rulers of the darkness of this age, and against the spiritual forces of wickedness in the heavenly places. Therefore put on the whole armor of God, that you may be able to withstand in the evil day, and having done all, to stand.

"Stand therefore, having the utility belt of truth buckled around your waist, and having put on the breastplate of righteousness, and having fitted your feet with the preparation of the Good News of peace, above all, taking up the shield of faith, with which you will be able to quench all the fiery darts of the evil one. And take the helmet of salvation, and the sword of the Spirit, which is the word of God; with all prayer and requests, praying at all times in the Spirit, and being watchful to this end in all perseverance and requests for all the saints" (Ephesians 6:10-18).

Chapter 2 Discussion Questions:
Knowing the Truth

1. What is God's expectation of His people?
2. Why is this a just expectation?
3. How much difference do surveys show between the world and the church when it comes to sinful living?
4. What is one of the most grievous sins being tolerated in the church today?
5. Because of this sin, what did Jude exhort the believers to do?
6. Who did Peter warn us about that would bring in destructive heresies, even denying the Master who bought them?
7. How would they exploit us?

Walking in the Light

8. Why do false teachers preach, "Peace, peace" when there is no peace?
9. When God looks at us, what does He see?
10. Why do some teach that you do not need to know Jesus as Lord?
11. Some teach that believers need to be under the law. What is the result for these believers?
12. What will the person that sows to the flesh reap?
13. What is the secret to being delivered from the deception of false teachings?
14. What was the purpose of our old man being crucified with Christ?
15. How do believers glorify God?
16. When a person commits sin, what does he become enslaved to?
17. Why are believers considered to be slaves of Christ?
18. Who is Peter speaking about when he says their last state is worse for them than the first?
19. What happens if someone purifies himself from false teachings?
20. What has God given every genuine believer to enable him to withstand false teachings?

Chapter 3

No Condemnation

If you are a genuine Christian, if you have been born from above and the Spirit of Christ dwells in you, that indwelling Holy Spirit will teach you all things. John assures us saying, "And as for you, the anointing which you received from Him remains in you, and you have no need for anyone to teach you; but as His anointing teaches you about all things, and is true and is not a lie, and just as it has taught you, you remain in Him" (1 John 2:27).

When we were born again we became new creations in Christ. Paul declares, "Therefore if anyone is in Christ, this person is a new creation; the old things passed away; behold, new things have come" (2 Corinthians 5:17).

Having been placed in Christ by God, we have received so many incredible blessings. Paul says, "Now we have not received the spirit of the world, but the Spirit who is from God, so that we may know the things freely given to us by God" (1 Corinthians 2:12). God gave us His Spirit to teach us, that we might know the blessings that have been freely given to us in Christ Jesus our Lord.

Paul explains in the first chapter of Galatians that he was not taught the gospel by men but by revelation from Jesus Christ. "For I would have you know, brothers and sisters, that the gospel which was preached by me is not of human invention. For I neither received it from man, nor was I taught it, but I received it through a revelation of Jesus Christ" (Galatians 1:11-12). How much of the gospel have you received by revelation from Jesus Christ?

Walking in the Light

Nearly everything we have learned about the gospel has been taught to us by men, not by revelation from Jesus Christ. We were taught by men who were taught by men who were taught by men.

Because we have experienced so little revelation, because we have experienced so little teaching directly by the indwelling Holy Spirit, we have a very limited understanding of the scriptures. The typical Christian today is virtually ignorant of the scriptures. Most of what we know is what some person has told us. And most of what we have been taught has never been challenged.

With much of what we have been taught, we have never attempted to verify by searching the scriptures to see if those teachings are true or false. Therefore, we, the church, have become very susceptible to being led astray by false teachings. In fact, it seems that many of the teachings being preached in the churches today are false teachings. Many of these false teachings have severely undermined the faith of the believers. Many of these teachings seem to be designed to make professing Christians feel better about themselves and about how they are living their lives preaching "Peace, Peace!" when there is no peace.

Let us now look to the Holy Spirit to teach us what Paul meant when that same Holy Spirit directed him to write the first verse of the eighth chapter of the letter to the church in Rome. In Romans 8:1 Paul wrote, "Therefore no condemnation now exists for those who are Christ Jesus" (HCSB).

What meaning did the Spirit intend to communicate by the use of the word "condemnation" in this verse? Paul's letter to the church in Rome was originally written in the ancient Greek language. Therefore, to begin our quest to understand this verse we can examine the meaning of the Greek word that was translated as condemnation. We can also review how the various other translations interpreted that Greek word. Most importantly, we can examine the context in which that word was used in this verse as well as wherever else it was used in other passages of scripture.

Paul, in writing to the church in Ephesus, prays "that the God of our Lord Jesus Christ, the Father of glory, may give you a spirit of wisdom and of revelation in the knowledge of Him" (Ephesians 1:17). May God grant us that same spirit of wisdom and revelation now as we look to Him for real understanding.

A popular teaching in many churches is based on understanding the word condemnation in Romans 8:1 to mean guilt or blame. They interpret the word condemnation here to refer to emotions or feelings. Thus, they understand this verse to say, "Therefore no guilt or blame now exists for those who are in Christ Jesus."

In order to support this interpretation, they teach that when a person gets saved, all their sins, past, present and future are forgiven. If all sins, past, present, and future have been forgiven, the believer should never again feel any condemnation or guilt because they are in Christ. If they do feel guilt or blame when they sin, that condemnation is from the devil. It is the enemy accusing them. If they accept his accusation, they are doubting the effectiveness of the death of Christ on the cross for their sins and the effectiveness of His blood to take away those sins.

As a consequence, they teach that when God looks at them, He doesn't see them as they really are, but He sees Jesus. They are covered over with His robe of righteousness.

They freely admit that they live sinful lives. In fact, they say they sin all the time, many times every day. They justify their life of sin by teaching that it is normal. It is the expected experience for a Christian.

They use chapter 7 of the book of Romans as their gold standard for how a Christian is expected to live. They teach that Romans 7:13-24 is Paul's personal testimony of his life as a Christian when he states that he is enslaved to sin, that he has no ability to do the good that he wants to do, and that he practices the evil that he hates.

Walking in the Light

It is because of recent encounters with these and similar teachings that I have sought the Lord for understanding of Romans 8:1 and of Romans chapter seven. I have asked the Lord to teach me what the word translated as condemnation actually means based on the meaning of the Greek word used in the original writings of Paul, and on the context within which he used that Greek word.

I have also asked the Lord to teach me what the Holy Spirit, through Paul, was attempting to communicate to us in chapter seven. Was he referring to his experience as a Christian? Or was he referring to his experience as a merely natural man, an unspiritual man, that had encountered the law of God and had agreed in his mind that the law was good, and had set out to do that good that he saw in the law?

Within the next four chapters of this book, I will attempt to set forth what the Lord has shown me concerning these matters. We will begin this journey together by examining the meaning of the Greek word that has been translated almost universally as condemnation.

The Greek word that has been translated as condemnation is "katakrima" We find, according to "Strongs Exhaustive Concordance," that this particular Greek word was used only three times in the entire Bible. All three times were in this one letter of Paul to the church in Rome. It is used once here in the first verse of the eighth chapter of Romans and twice in the fifth chapter of this same letter.

According to "Strong's," the Greek word #2631, katakrima, means "an adverse sentence." Here Paul is speaking in a legal sense. He has in mind a person that has committed a crime, an offense, and has therefore been brought to court to appear before the judge. An accusation has been made and the evidence is presented. The court, the judge, then weighs the evidence and arrives at a judgment.

The judgment, the verdict, of the court is announced, either innocent or guilty. If the accused is determined by the court to be guilty, then sentence is passed. The guilty person is then sentenced by the court, condemned to death, or condemned to

20 years in prison, or some other specific adverse sentence. This condemnation is an adverse sentence. It is a sentence passed against the guilty person that must be carried out until or unless an acquittal or a pardon is received setting the prisoner free.

Here Paul is using the word condemnation to refer to an adverse sentence that was passed against a guilty offender. However, he is not using it in a general sense of just any condemnation. He is using it to refer to a very specific condemnation, a very specific adverse sentence handed down by the court on the occasion of the judgment of a specific person found guilty of a very specific offence.

In order to understand what this condemnation, this specific adverse sentence is, we need to understand who the guilty person was and what the specific offense was. In order to arrive at a correct understanding, we need to consider the immediate context of the passages where this Greek word katakrima is used.

The word, katakrima, translated as condemnation, appears in chapter five, verses sixteen and eighteen. The context in which it appears is as follows: "Therefore, just as sin entered the world through one man, and death through sin, in this way death spread to all men, because all sinned . . . death reigned from Adam to Moses, even over those who did not sin in the likeness of Adam's transgression . . . the gift is not like the one man's sin, because from one sin came the judgment, resulting in condemnation (an adverse sentence), but from many trespasses came the gift, resulting in justification . . . So then, as through one trespass there is condemnation (an adverse sentence) for everyone, so also through one righteous act there is life-giving justification for everyone. For just as through one man's disobedience the many were made sinners, so also through the one man's obedience the many will be made righteous" (Romans 5:12-19).

Here Paul is speaking in very particular terms. He is referring to one person who sinned and upon whose sin judgment was passed resulting in condemnation. The condemnation, however, was not just upon the one man that sinned, but upon all men. "So then as through one trespass, all men were condemned." Paul is referring to one person that sinned resulting in condemnation, an adverse sentence, being passed upon all men, all people. "By the trespass of the one, death reigned through the one."

"Through the one man's disobedience many were made sinners." Who was this person that sinned resulting in condemnation to all men?

Paul explains, "Wherefore as by one man sin entered into this world, and by sin death; and so death passed upon all men, in whom all have sinned" (Romans 5:12, DRA). Who is this one man in whom all have sinned?

Paul goes on in verse 14 to reveal to us who the one man was whose transgression resulted in condemnation unto all men. "Nevertheless death reigned from Adam until Moses, even over those whose sins weren't like Adam's disobedience" (Romans 5:14).

It was Adam who sinned. It was in his sin, in his disobedience, that all were constituted as sinners. "Through the one man's disobedience many were made sinners" (Romans 5:19).

What was the specific adverse sentence, the specific condemnation, that resulted in not just Adam, but all men being made sinners as a result of the one man's sin? We need to get a better understanding of the mind of the judge in this case in order to understand the adverse sentence he passed.

Jesus Christ our Lord reveals this mind of God, the righteous judge, to us. He specifically reveals God's mind concerning this adverse sentence that was passed against Adam for his sin. In John chapter eight we are enlightened by Jesus during His conversation with the Jews who had believed in Him.

"So Jesus was saying to those Jews who had believed Him, 'If you continue in My word, then you are truly My disciples; and you will know the truth, and the truth will set you free.' They answered Him, 'We are Abraham's descendants and have never been enslaved to anyone; how is it that You say, "You will become free"?'

"Jesus answered them, 'Truly, truly I say to you, everyone who commits sin is a slave of sin . . . So if the Son sets you free, you really will be free'" (John 8:30-36).

Jesus told these Jews that had believed in Him, that if they would continue in His word they would know the truth and the truth would set them free. The Jews rightly understood that Jesus was telling them that they were slaves. He was telling them that they had been enslaved and did not even realize it.

The Jews proved they did not realize their enslavement by insisting that they had never been enslaved to anyone. Jesus therefore explained to them the reality of their enslavement saying, "Everyone who commits sin is a slave of sin." This was the truth that the Jews did not understand. They were slaves to sin.

When Adam sinned in the Garden of Eden by disobeying God's commandment not to eat of the fruit of the Tree of the Knowledge of Good and Evil, God judged Adam. Finding him guilty of sinning, God condemned Adam based on this truth that Jesus revealed to the Jews that were believing in Him.

Jesus said, "Everyone who commits sin is a slave of sin." This truth was the basis that God used in His condemnation, His adverse sentence, that He passed against Adam as a result of his transgression.

Because Adam sinned, God condemned Adam to be enslaved to sin. Thus Adam, and all mankind in Adam, became enslaved to sin and were thereby made sinners. All mankind, as a result of God's condemnation, became enslaved to sin.

God condemned Adam, and all mankind in him, to slavery to sin. This was God's condemnation, His adverse sentence, that He passed against Adam. As slaves of sin, all mankind were constituted to be sinners by nature. That is what fallen mankind does, they sin because they are sinners.

Therefore, all have sinned (Romans 3:23). Paul tells us in Romans 6:23 that the wages of sin is death. The penalty of sin is death. "Therefore, just as sin entered the world through one man, and death through sin, in this way death spread to all men, because all sinned. 2 Chronicles 25:4 states,"Every man shall die for his own sin."

However, Jesus revealed to the Jews, not only that they were slaves to sin but, that if they would continue in His word, they would know the truth and the truth would set them free. He told them, "So if the Son sets you free, you really will be free."

How would they be set free? In Romans chapter five verses sixteen and eighteen, Paul reveals the secret of this freedom that Christ promised. Here Paul uses the Greek words translated as justification.

The word justification appears only three times in the King James Version of the New Testament. It appears once in Romans 5:16 and once in Romans 5:18. The third occurrence is in Romans 4:25.

The Greek word translated as justification in Romans 4:25 and 5:18 is dikaiosis, which means acquittal. The Greek word translated as justification in Romans 5:16 is dikaioma, which means a decision to render innocent.

"And the gift is not like the one man's sin, because from one sin came the judgment, resulting in condemnation (an adverse sentence), but from many trespasses came the gift, resulting in justification (being rendered innocent, being freed). Since by the one man's trespass, death reigned through that one man, how much more will those who receive the overflow of grace and the gift of righteousness (having been rendered innocent, holy) reign in life through the one man, Jesus Christ.

"So then, as through one trespass there is condemnation (an adverse sentence) for everyone, so also through one righteous act there is life-giving justification (acquittal) for everyone. For just as through one man's disobedience the many were made sinners, so also through the one man's obedience the many will be made righteous (innocent, holy)" (Romans 5:16-19, HCSB).

Paul tells us in Romans 4:25, "He (Jesus) was delivered up for our trespasses and raised for our justification." Jesus was delivered up, crucified, dying on the cross as our substitute for our sins. He died in our place, paying the price for our sins.

Jesus was also raised from the dead for our justification. God demonstrated His approval of Jesus's holy life and sacrificial death by raising Jesus from the dead. Through God's acceptance of Jesus's death for us, as payment for our sins, we who trust in Him are rendered innocent and are set free from the condemnation of slavery to sin.

Paul explains, "For since by a man death came, by a man also came the resurrection of the dead. For as in Adam all die, so also in Christ all will be made alive. But each in his own order: Christ the first fruits, after that those who are Christ's at His coming" (1 Corinthians 15:21-23, NASB).

"Therefore, no condemnation now exists for those in Christ Jesus, because the Spirit's law of life in Christ Jesus has set you free from the law of sin and of death" (Romans 8:1-2, HCSB). "For as in Adam all die, so also in Christ all will be made alive." Through Christ's death and resurrection, we who are in Christ have been set free from the law of sin and of death. We have been set free from bondage to sin, now in this life, and will be made alive with Christ at His coming!

According to John, "Anyone who believes in Him (Jesus) is not condemned, but anyone who does not believe is already condemned, because he has not believed in the name of the One and Only Son of God" (John 3:18, HCSB). Only those that have, by faith, believed in Jesus Christ, the Son of God, have been freed (acquitted, rendered innocent) from the condemnation of slavery to sin.

It is this condemnation that Paul says no longer exists for those who are in Christ Jesus. Romans 8:1 in this context actually means, "Therefore there is now no enslavement to sin for those who are in Christ Jesus." Those in Christ are no longer slaves to sin. They have been liberated.

Paul writes, "Apart from the law, God's righteousness has been revealed—attested by the Law and the Prophets —that is, God's righteousness through faith in Jesus Christ, to all who believe, since there is no distinction. For all have sinned and fall short of the glory of God. They are justified freely (rendered innocent) by His grace through the redemption that is in Christ Jesus . . . in His restraint God passed over the sins previously committed. God presented Him (Jesus) to demonstrate His righteousness at the present time, so that He would be righteous (holy) and declare righteous (holy) the one who has faith in Jesus" (Romans 3:21-26).

The point Paul is making in Romans 8:1 is a summation of the case he presented in the preceding passage from the middle of Romans chapter five through chapter seven. Those that are in Christ Jesus have been set free. They are no longer slaves to sin. Sin no longer has dominion over them. They have been set free to serve God in newness of life.

By the entire context, Paul makes it clear that his use of the word (katakrima) condemnation has nothing to do with feelings, especially feelings of guilt over sin. If anyone in Christ Jesus sins, they should and will experience feelings of guilt, unless their consciences have been seared by repeated refusal to heed the Spirit's conviction and call to repentance.

Chapter 3 Discussion Questions:
No Condemnation

1. What have believers been given that teaches them all things?
2. How did Paul receive the gospel he preached?
3. How have most believers been taught about the gospel?
4. Why do most believers have a very limited understanding of the scriptures?
5. Why has the church become so susceptible to being led astray by false teachings?

6. What effect are many false teachings designed to have of professing Christians?
7. What is taught to support the idea that condemnation in Romans 1 is about emotions?
8. For those that believe this teaching, what is the source of any guilt or blame?
9. To support these teachings, what do they say God sees when He looks at us?
10. How do these believers justify living lives of continual sin?
11. What is the Greek word translated as condemnation in Romans 8:1?
12. What does the Greek word katakrima mean?
13. In what sense does Paul use the word condemnation?
14. What is an adverse sentence?
15. Who sinned resulting in condemnation to all men?
16. What was the specific adverse sentence that resulted in all men being constituted as sinners?
17. As a result of the condemnation that God passed against Adam, who became enslaved to sin?
18. What does Romans 4:25 mean, "Jesus was raised to our justification?
19. What does Romans 8:1 in this legal context actually mean?
20. What is Paul's point in his summation of Romans chapters 5-7?

Chapter 4

Set Free to Walk by the Spirit

As we just learned in the previous chapter, slavery to sin is the condemnation that Paul says no longer exists for those who are in Christ Jesus. Properly translated, Romans 8:1 should read, "Therefore there is now no enslavement to sin for those who are in Christ Jesus."

This is strongly supported by Paul's discourse in Romans chapter six. "For we know that our old self was crucified with Him in order that sin's dominion over the body may be abolished, so that we may no longer be enslaved to sin, since a person who has died is freed from sin's claims. Therefore do not let sin reign in your mortal body, so that you obey its desires" (Romans 6:6-7, 12).

Paul continues, "Don't you know that if you offer yourselves to someone as obedient slaves, you are slaves of that one you obey—either of sin leading to death or of obedience leading to righteousness? But thank God that, although you used to be slaves of sin, you obeyed from the heart that pattern of teaching you were transferred to, and having been liberated from sin, you became enslaved to righteousness" (Romans 6:16-18).

Paul concludes his argument saying, "For just as you offered the parts of yourselves as slaves to moral impurity, and to greater and greater lawlessness, so now offer them as slaves to righteousness, which results in sanctification. For when you were slaves of sin, you were free from allegiance to righteousness. So what fruit was produced then from the things you are now ashamed of? For the end of those things is death. But now, since you have been liberated from sin and have become enslaved to God, you have your fruit, which results in sanctification—and the end is eternal life!" (Romans 6:19-22, HCSB).

These verses are all from Romans chapter six. I do not believe that the Holy Spirit writing through Paul could have possibly made it any clearer. As a result of one man's sin, Adam's sin, all mankind became enslaved to sin. The only way to be liberated, the only way to be set free from this slavery to sin is by the truth setting us free.

Who or what is the truth that sets us free from slavery to sin? Jesus said in John 14:6, "I am the way, the truth, and the life; no one comes to the Father except through Me." Jesus is the truth that sets us free from slavery to sin. "So if the Son sets you free, you really will be free'" (John 8:36).

Praise God! As genuine born-again Christians, not only are all of our past sins forgiven, but even more glorious, we are no longer enslaved to sin. Sin no longer has dominion over those that are in Christ. By Christ's death and resurrection, genuine Christians have been set free from bondage to sin.

We have been set free from bondage to sin leading to death, and have been enslaved to God resulting in sanctification, the end of which is eternal life. We are no longer forced by the sin in our flesh to practice the evil that we do not want to do. Now as believers, we only sin when we choose to, when we are drawn away and enticed by our own evil desires. As James says, "Each one is tempted when he is drawn away by his own lust and enticed" (James 1:14).

This is why it is so important that we control what we think about. Paul exhorts us, "Therefore, if you have been raised with Christ, keep seeking the things that are above, where Christ is, seated at the right hand of God. Set your minds on the things that are above, not on the things that are on earth. For you have died, and your life is hidden with Christ in God" (Colossians 3:1-3).

Paul continues, "Finally brothers, whatever is true, whatever is honorable, whatever is just, whatever is pure,

Walking in the Light

whatever is lovely, whatever is commendable—if there is any moral excellence and if there is any praise—dwell on these things" (Philippians 4:8, HCSB). If we think about these things, we will act accordingly. The thoughts we dwell on lead to the actions we take.

It is because of this truth, those that are in Christ Jesus are no longer enslaved to sin, that we are expected by God to live holy lives. Genuine Christians are no longer slaves of sin. We are now slaves of God resulting in sanctification. Because sin no longer has dominion over us, we are now free to serve God in newness of life. We begin this life of serving God by setting our minds on the Spirit.

We are empowered by the law of the Spirit of life in Christ Jesus. It has set us free from the law of sin and of death. "For the law of the Spirit of life in Christ Jesus has set you free from the law of sin and of death" (Romans 8:2). We are free, not to live according to the flesh, but to live according to the Spirit. Therefore, we must set our minds not on the things of the flesh, but on the Spirit and the things of the Spirit

Paul explains, "For what the Law could not do, weak as it was through the flesh, God did: sending His own Son in the likeness of sinful flesh and as an offering for sin, He condemned sin in the flesh, so that the requirement of the Law might be fulfilled in us who do not walk according to the flesh but according to the Spirit. For those who are in accord with the flesh set their minds on the things of the flesh, but those who are in accord with the Spirit, the things of the Spirit. For the mind set on the flesh is death, but the mind set on the Spirit is life and peace, because the mind set on the flesh is hostile toward God; for it does not subject itself to the law of God, for it is not even able to do so, and those who are in the flesh cannot please God.

"However, you are not in the flesh but in the Spirit, if indeed the Spirit of God dwells in you. But if anyone does not have the Spirit of Christ, he does not belong to Him. If Christ is in you, though the body is dead because of sin, yet the spirit is alive because of righteousness. But if the Spirit of Him who raised Jesus from the dead dwells in you, He who raised Christ Jesus from the dead will also give life to your mortal bodies through His Spirit who dwells in you.

"So then, brothers and sisters, we are under obligation, not to the flesh, to live according to the flesh— for if you are living in accord with the flesh, you are going to die; but if by the Spirit you are putting to death the deeds of the body, you will live. For all who are being led by the Spirit of God, these are sons and daughters of God. For you have not received a spirit of slavery leading to fear again, but you have received a spirit of adoption as sons and daughters by which we cry out, "Abba! Father!" The Spirit Himself testifies with our spirit that we are children of God, and if children, heirs also, heirs of God and fellow heirs with Christ, if indeed we suffer with Him so that we may also be glorified with Him" (Romans 8:3-17, NASB).

Could God have made it any clearer? Christians are expected to live holy lives in obedience to the leading of the indwelling Holy Spirit. John affirms, "This is how we are sure that we have come to know Him: by keeping His commands. The one who says, 'I have come to know Him,' yet doesn't keep His commands, is a liar, and the truth is not in him. But whoever keeps His word, truly in him the love of God is perfected. This is how we know we are in Him: The one who says he remains in Him should walk just as He walked" (1 John 2:3-6).

Peter urges us, "Therefore, prepare your minds for action, keep sober in spirit, set your hope completely on the grace to be brought to you at the revelation of Jesus Christ. As obedient children, do not be conformed to the former lusts which were yours in your ignorance, but like the Holy One who called you, be holy yourselves also in all your behavior; because it is written: 'YOU SHALL BE HOLY, FOR I AM HOLY'" (1 Peter 1:13-16).

Again Paul exhorts us, "Christ has liberated us to be free. Stand firm then and don't submit again to a yoke of slavery. . . For you were called to be free, brothers; only don't use this freedom as an opportunity for the flesh, but serve one another through love. For the entire law is fulfilled in one statement: Love your neighbor as yourself. But if you bite and devour one another, watch out, or you will be consumed by one another.

"I say then, walk by the Spirit and you will not carry out the desire of the flesh. For the flesh desires what is against the Spirit, and the Spirit desires what is against the flesh; these are opposed to each other, so that you don't do what you want. But if you are led by the Spirit, you are not under the law.

"Now the works of the flesh are obvious: sexual immorality, moral impurity, promiscuity, idolatry, sorcery, hatreds, strife, jealousy, outbursts of anger, selfish ambitions, dissensions, factions, envy, drunkenness, carousing, and anything similar. I tell you about these things in advance – as I told you before – that those who practice such things will not inherit the kingdom of God.

"But the fruit of the Spirit is love, joy, peace, patience, kindness, goodness, faith, gentleness, self-control. Against such things there is no law. Now those who belong to Christ Jesus have crucified the flesh with its passions and desires. Since we live by the Spirit, we must also follow the Spirit" (Galatians 5:1, 13-25, HCSB).

This is not saying that genuine Christians cannot or will not ever sin. The sin that dwells within our flesh cannot force the believer to sin. According to James, if a believer sins, it is because he "is tempted when he is drawn away and enticed by his own evil desires. Then after desire has conceived, it gives birth to sin, and when sin is fully grown, it gives birth to death" (James 1:14-15, HCSB).

The believer becomes a new creation when he is born again. When the Spirit of Christ comes to indwell the believer, the believer's spirit is made alive. He is now able to have fellowship with God who is Spirit.

With his spirit made alive, the believer now has two natures within him competing for his attention. He still has the old fallen sin nature, the sin that dwells in his flesh. Now, he also has a new nature, the Spirit of Christ indwelling his spirit. These two natures within the believer are opposed to each other.

Now the born-again believer has a choice, every day, every moment. Will he live according to the flesh, or will he live according to the Spirit? As we saw in the passage above, Paul reminds us, "Walk by the Spirit and you will not carry out the desire of the flesh. For the flesh desires what is against the Spirit, and the Spirit desires what is against the flesh; these are opposed to each other, so that you don't do what you want. But if you are led by the Spirit, you are not under the law."

Our ability to walk according to the Spirit is very much dependent on how we think. We must set our minds on the things of the Spirit. We must not allow our minds to dwell on the flesh and the things of the flesh. We must take "every thought captive to the obedience of Christ" (2 Corinthians 10:5).

It is our thoughts, the things that we think about and dwell on, that result in our actions. Our minds are the real battleground of this spiritual war that we are in. What do you allow yourself to think about, the things of the flesh or the things of the Spirit?

Galatians 5:16 is one of the greatest promises in all of scripture, "Walk by the Spirit and you will not carry out the desire of the flesh." This is how powerfully the Spirit is working within us. If we are walking according to the Spirit, the flesh does not have a chance, we will not fulfill its lusts.

Paul prays for the believers in the church in Ephesus that "The eyes of your heart may be enlightened, so that you will know what is the hope of His calling, what are the riches of the glory of His inheritance in the saints, and what is the boundless greatness of His power toward us who believe. These are in accordance with the working of the strength of His might."

He is praying that we would understand the incredible power of the Spirit of Christ working in us to transform us, to conform us to His image, that we would be enabled to walk

Walking in the Light

just as he walked, being led and empowered by the Holy Spirit to live lives that are pleasing to God.

This corresponds with what Paul wrote to the church in Rome. "For those who live according to the flesh think about the things of the flesh, but those who live according to the Spirit, about the things of the Spirit. For the mind-set of the flesh is death, but the mind-set of the Spirit is life and peace. . . So then, brothers, we are not obligated to the flesh to live according to the flesh, for if you live according to the flesh, you are going to die. But if by the Spirit you put to death the deeds of the body, you will live. All those led by God's Spirit are God's sons" (Romans 8:5-6, 12-14).

The believer is no longer a slave to sin. Sin no longer has dominion over him. He has been set free, liberated by the Son, Jesus Christ our Lord. He now has the freedom to choose to be led by the flesh or by the Spirit.

However, if the believer chooses to live according to the flesh, God will not be pleased with him. He will experience condemnation and guilt. Here is where the false teachings from Romans 8:1 come in. They teach that because the blood that Christ shed by His death for us on the cross, our sins have been forgiven, all of our sins, past, present and future. This, they say, is why there is now then no condemnation, no guilt and no blame for those in Christ.

These false teachers claim that a believer should never experience any condemnation, never experience any sense of God's displeasure with us when we sin. They have taken a term, condemnation, that Paul used in a strictly legal sense and changed it into an emotionally based term. Some teach that there is no need to repent of sin after being saved because all our sins were already forgiven the moment we believed.

Some even insist that God is pleased with us because He is pleased with Jesus whom we accepted as our savior. God loves us, they say, and is pleased with us no matter how we live. He will never condemn us. Because of this twisted interpretation of the word condemnation, they say that if we ever feel any guilt or condemnation for our sins, it is because we are not trusting in Christ's blood that was shed for us.

The King James Version and some other early translations of Romans include the phrase, "Who walk not after the flesh, but after the Spirit," as part of Romans 8:1. In the King James Version it reads, "There is therefore now no condemnation to them which are in Christ Jesus, who walk not after the flesh, but after the Spirit."

Recent translations have removed this phrase claiming that the oldest manuscripts did not have this phrase as a part of verse one. However, this exact phrase appears in verse four. "That the righteousness of the law might be fulfilled in us, who walk not after the flesh, but after the Spirit."

I believe that the Holy Spirit, guiding Paul in his writing, knew that false teachers would twist and pervert the meaning of verse one and used the following verses to give context to clarify how vitally important how we live and think is. It is not enough just to be born of the Spirit. We must also walk according to the leading of the Spirit. A believer can only experience peace with God when he is walking according to the Spirit.

"For those who live according to the flesh think about the things of the flesh, but those who live according to the Spirit, about the things of the Spirit. For the mind-set of the flesh is death, but the mind-set of the Spirit is life and peace."

If we walk according to the flesh, fulfilling its lusts, God will not be pleased with us. He makes this perfectly clear in verse eight, "Those who are in the flesh cannot please God." God is displeased with believers whenever they are walking according to the flesh. May I go so far as to say that God is angry with us when we are walking according to the flesh.

Whenever we are walking according to the flesh we should experience conviction, condemnation, guilt and blame. We should feel shame. We should feel guilty of, at the very least, disappointing our heavenly Father. Whenever we are walking according to the flesh, we should be keenly aware of our

Walking in the Light

Father's disappointment with us. We cannot have peace with God until we repent and turn back to Him.

These false teachings are deceiving God's people, telling them, "Peace, peace!" when there is no peace. These false teachings are Satanic, straight from the enemy. As Jesus said to Peter, ""Get behind Me, Satan! You are an offense to Me because you're not thinking about God's concerns, but man's" (Matthew 16:23, HCSB). This is exactly what these false teachers are doing. They are thinking about the concerns of man, not about God's.

The apostle John wrote to believers in 1 John 1:5-2:2 saying, "Now this is the message we have heard from Him and declare to you: God is light, and there is absolutely no darkness in Him. If we say, 'We have fellowship with Him,' yet we walk in darkness, we are lying and are not practicing the truth.

"But if we walk in the light as He Himself is in the light, we have fellowship with one another, and the blood of Jesus His Son cleanses us from all sin. If we say, 'We have no sin,' we are deceiving ourselves, and the truth is not in us. If we confess our sins, He is faithful and righteous to forgive us our sins and to cleanse us from all unrighteousness. If we say, "We don't have any sin," we make Him a liar, and His word is not in us.

"My little children, I am writing you these things so that you may not sin. But if anyone does sin, we have an advocate with the Father—Jesus Christ the Righteous One. He Himself is the propitiation for our sins, and not only for ours, but also for those of the whole world" (HCSB).

John continues writing to believers in 1 John 2:3-6, "This is how we are sure that we have come to know Him: by keeping His commands. The one who says, "I have come to know Him," yet doesn't keep His commands, is a liar, and the truth is not in him. But whoever keeps His word, truly in him the love of God is perfected. This is how we know we are in Him: The one who says he remains in Him should walk just as He walked."

God expects us to live holy lives, pleasing to Him, worthy of the kingdom. He did not send Jesus into the world just to die on the cross so that our sins would be forgiven. Forgiveness of sins was available before Jesus came, even before He shed His blood dying on the cross for us.

Much more than this, God sent Jesus into the world to set us free from bondage to sin. God sent Jesus into the world to deliver us from Satan's power, to set us free. He set us free to serve Him. We serve Him by allowing the Spirit to lead us and empower us to live lives free from sinning.

Remember Paul's words in Romans chapter 5, "For if, while we were enemies, we were reconciled to God through the death of His Son, then how much more, having been reconciled, will we be saved by His life!" This is the much more! We are not just forgiven, we are saved, delivered, set free from the dominion of sin. We are saved by the power of His life indwelling us as the Holy Spirit in our spirit.

If a Christian should happen to fall into sin, as soon as he realizes the error of his way, he must stop sinning and repent. He must confess his sin and turn back to God trusting in the power of the blood of Christ to cleanse him from his sin. If we refuse to acknowledge and confess our sin, "we are deceiving ourselves, and the truth is not in us. If we confess our sins, He is faithful and righteous to forgive us our sins and to cleanse us from all unrighteousness."

If we sin, we must repent. Sin must be dealt with in a serious and thorough manner. God hates sin. God is not pleased with anyone that is living in sin. That does not mean that God has stopped loving us. It does mean that God is not mocked.

Do not deceive yourself. Do not be conceited. You will reap what you sow. God takes sin seriously and He judges sin severely.

Paul warns us, "Do not be conceited, but fear; for if God did not spare the natural branches, He will not spare you, either. See then the kindness and severity of God: to those who fell, severity, but to you, God's kindness, if you continue in

His kindness; for otherwise you too will be cut off" (Romans 11:20-22).

Again we are warned, "Do not be deceived, God is not mocked; for whatever a person sows, this he will also reap. For the one who sows to his own flesh will reap destruction from the flesh, but the one who sows to the Spirit will reap eternal life from the Spirit. Let's not become discouraged in doing good, for in due time we will reap, if we do not become weary. So then, while we have opportunity, let's do good to all people, and especially to those who are of the household of the faith" (Galatians 6:7-10).

Chapter 4 Discussion Questions:
Set Free to Walk by the Spirit

1. Properly translated, how should Romans 8:1 read?
2. Why was our old self crucified with Christ?
3. What happens when we let sin reign in our mortal body?
4. When we are liberated from sin, what do we become enslaved to?
5. What is the end result of sanctification?
6. If believers are no longer slaves of sin, when do we sin?
7. Why is it so important to control what we think?
8. What does the mind set on the Spirit produce?
9. What are we to set our minds upon?
10. Why is it impossible for those that are in the flesh to please God?
11. How can we be sure that we have come to know Jesus?
12. Why are we, as born-again Christians, expected to be holy in all our behavior?
13. What is the one sure way not to carry out the desire of the flesh?
14. Who will inherit the kingdom of God?
15. What two natures are within the born-again believer opposing each other?

16. Why is it so important that we control what we think about?
17. What did Paul pray for the believers in the church in Ephesus?
18. What is the incredible power of the Spirit of Christ working in us to accomplish?
19. Who are God's sons?
20. What born-again believers is God not pleased with?
21. Why is it not enough just to be born of the Spirit?
22. Why was John writing to us in 1 John chapter 2?
23. Why did God send Jesus into the world?
24. What will we reap if we sow to the flesh?
25. What will we reap if we sow to the Spirit?

Chapter 5

A Wretched Man

In this chapter we will attempt to gain a better understanding of Romans chapter seven. We will begin by reviewing some of the things we learned in the previous chapters "No Condemnation" and "Set Free to Walk by the Spirit." In those chapters we learned that Adam sinned while in the Garden of Eden by disobeying God. "Nevertheless death reigned from Adam until Moses, even over those whose sins weren't like Adam's disobedience" (Romans 5:14, NASB).

It was Adam who sinned. It was through his disobedience that sin entered the world. "Wherefore as by one man sin entered into this world, and by sin death; and so death passed upon all men, in whom all have sinned" (Romans 5:12, DRA).

We were all in Adam when Adam sinned. Therefore, in him all have sinned. By that one person's sin, death has passed unto all men. Through this one man's trespass, all mankind were made sinners. It was in his sin, in his disobedience, that all were constituted as sinners.

"Through one trespass, all men were condemned; even so through one act of righteousness, all men were justified to life. For as through the one man's disobedience many were made sinners, even so through the obedience of the one, many will be made righteous" (Romans 5:19, NASB).

Adam's nature was fundamentally changed by this one sinful act of disobedience. His nature, his constitution, was changed from innocence to sinfulness. He was now constituted a sinner. That was now his nature.

"The gift is not like that which came through the one who sinned, for on the one hand the judgment arose from one offense, resulting in condemnation, but on the other hand the gracious gift arose from many offenses, resulting in justification. For if by the offense of the one, death reigned through the one, much more will those who receive the abundance of grace and of the gift of righteousness reign in life through the One, Jesus Christ. So then, as through one offense the result was condemnation to all mankind, so also through one act of righteousness the result was justification of life to all mankind" (Romans 5:16-18, NASB).

What was the specific condemnation that resulted in not just Adam, but all men being made sinners as a result of the one man's sin? Jesus reveals this to us in John chapter eight, during His conversation with the Jews who had believed in Him.

"Jesus was saying to those Jews who had believed Him, 'If you continue in my word, then you are truly My disciples and you will know the truth, and the truth will set you free.' They answered Him, 'We are Abraham's descendants and have never been enslaved to anyone; how is it that You say, "You will become free"?'

"Jesus answered them, 'Truly, truly I say to you, everyone who commits sin is a slave of sin. Now the slave does not remain in the house forever; the son does remain forever. So if the Son sets you free, you really will be free'" (John 8:31-36, NASB).

Jesus told these Jews that had believed in Him, that if they would continue in His word, they would know the truth and the truth would set them free. The Jews rightly understood that Jesus was telling them that they were slaves. He was telling them that they had been enslaved and did not even realize it.

The Jews proved they did not realize their enslavement by insisting that they had never been enslaved to anyone. Jesus therefore explained to them the reality of their enslavement saying, "Everyone who commits sin is a slave of sin." This was the truth that the Jews did not understand. They were slaves to sin.

When Adam sinned in the Garden of Eden by disobeying God's commandment not to eat of the fruit of the Tree of the Knowledge of Good and Evil, God judged Adam. Finding him guilty of sinning, God condemned Adam based on this truth, "Everyone who commits sin is a slave of sin."

This truth was the basis that God used in His condemnation. His adverse sentence passed against Adam as a result of his transgression was that Adam would become a slave to sin. Because Adam sinned, God condemned Adam to be enslaved to sin. Thus Adam, and all mankind in Adam, became enslaved to sin and were thereby made sinners. All mankind, as a result of God's condemnation, became enslaved to sin.

The disobedience of this one man, Adam, resulted in the adverse sentence, the condemnation of slavery to sin. Because Adam sinned, he became a sinner. Because he was now constituted a sinner by nature, he would just naturally sin. We will see this illustrated in greater detail as we study chapter seven of Romans.

The obedience, the one righteous act, of our Lord Jesus Christ was the source of the righteousness that resulted in justification and reconciliation. "And not only that, but we also rejoice in God through our Lord Jesus Christ, through whom we have now received this reconciliation" (Romans 5:11, HCSB). "Through one act of righteousness, all men were justified to life. . . Through the one man's obedience, many will be made righteous" (Romans 5:18-19, HCSB). This is illustrated in more detail in chapters six and eight of Romans.

In chapter six Paul is addressing the question, "Should we continue in sin?" We were living in sin before we were born again, before we got saved. Now, as born-again believers, the question is, "Should we continue in sin?"

Paul's answer is an unwavering, "Absolutely not! How can we who died to sin still live in it? Or are you unaware that all of us who were baptized into Christ Jesus were baptized into His death? Therefore we were buried with Him by baptism into death, in order that, just as Christ was raised from the dead by the glory of the Father, so we too may walk in a new way of life.

"For if we have been joined with Him in the likeness of His death, we will certainly also be in the likeness of His resurrection. For we know that our old self was crucified with Him in order that sin's dominion over the body may be abolished, so that we may no longer be enslaved to sin, since a person who has died is freed from sin's claims" (Romans 6:2-7, HCSB).

In essence, Paul is asking the brothers, "Don't you understand? When a believer is baptized into Christ Jesus, he is, by the Spirit, baptized into Christ's death. By our death with Christ, sin's dominion over the body has been abolished. We are no longer enslaved to sin. Death has freed us from sin's claims"

Just as in Adam, all sinned and thereby all were constituted sinners and were condemned to be slaves of sin as long as they lived. So also, we were in Christ, crucified with Him, so that through His death, we also would be dead to sin, but through the power of His resurrection we would be alive to God.

"Now if we died with Christ, we believe that we will also live with Him, because we know that Christ, having been raised from the dead, will not die again. Death no longer rules over Him. For in light of the fact that He died, He died to sin once for all; but in light of the fact that He lives, He lives to God. So, you too consider yourselves dead to sin but alive to God in Christ Jesus" (Romans 6:8-11, HCSB).

What freedom! What liberation! Through baptism, by the Holy Spirit, into Christ's death, we have been set free. We are no longer slaves of sin. We are no longer obligated to let sin reign in our mortal bodies so that we obey its desires. As those that are alive from the dead, we offer ourselves to God.

"Therefore do not let sin reign in your mortal body, so that you obey its desires. And do not offer any parts of it to sin as weapons for unrighteousness. But as those who are alive from the dead, offer yourselves to God, and all the parts of yourselves to God as weapons for righteousness. For sin will not rule over you, because you are not under law but under grace" (Romans 6:12-14, NASB).

In chapter seven, Paul illustrates how this condemnation of slavery to sin operates in the life of the person that is under the law. Not having Christ's life within, this person has no choice. He must walk according to the flesh resulting in death.

Even though this person delights in the law of God in his mind, he is not able to do the good that he wants to do because the sin in his flesh is warring against him and taking him captive, holding him in bondage, in slavery to sin. Chapter seven is all about the war within the person that in his mind loves the law of God, yet in his flesh is unable to do the good that is in that law because he is overpowered and enslaved by the sin in his flesh.

Paul begins Romans chapter seven by telling us that he is speaking to brothers, but not just any brothers. He is speaking to brothers that know the law. He is asking them, "Don't you realize that the law has authority over you until you die? Or don't you know, brothers (for I speak to men who know the law), that the law has dominion over a man for as long as he lives?" (Romans 7:1).

Paul is continuing to stress to these brothers the extreme importance of our death with Christ. It is through our death with Christ that we are not just freed from slavery to sin, but also freed from the law.

"Therefore, my brothers, you also were made dead to the law through the body of Christ, that you would be joined to another, to him who was raised from the dead, that we might produce fruit to God. For when we were in the flesh, the sinful passions which were through the law worked in our members to bring out fruit to death. But now we have been discharged from the law, having died to that in which we were held; so that we serve in newness of the spirit, and not in oldness of the letter." (Romans 7:4-6).

Paul is reminding the brothers, "All of us who were baptized into Christ Jesus were baptized into His death." He is encouraging them, "Consider yourselves dead to sin but alive to God in Christ Jesus" It is through the truth of this death that we are set free.

We must know our death with Christ in order to be able to confidently consider ourselves as dead to sin. It is only then that we can enter into the reality of being dead to sin, free from its dominion over us in our daily lives.

Our death to sin is not based on our feelings. Our death to sin is based on the fact that when we were baptized by the Holy Spirit into Christ, we were baptized into His death. We were crucified with Him. It is for this reason that we can consider ourselves dead to sin and alive to God.

Paul then asks the brothers, "Is the law bad? Is there a problem with the law?" His answer to his own question is adamant. "Absolutely not! The law is good. The law is spiritual. However, when the law came, it exposed and magnified the sin within me, and made it appear exceedingly sinful."

Paul is explaining to them God's purpose with the law. The law is a teacher, a schoolmaster, our guardian to bring us to Christ (Galatians 3:23-24). We might think that we are alright. But when the law comes, it exposes the sin that is within us and reveals to us how desperately we need deliverance. It reveals how desperately we need Jesus Christ as our Lord and Savior.

"What shall we say then? Is the law sin? May it never be! However, I wouldn't have known sin, except through the law. For I wouldn't have known coveting, unless the law had said, 'You shall not covet.' But sin, finding occasion through the commandment, produced in me all kinds of coveting. For apart from the law, sin is dead. I was alive apart from the law once, but when the commandment came, sin revived, and I died. The commandment which was for life, this I found to be for death; for sin, finding occasion through the commandment, deceived me, and through it killed me. Therefore the law indeed is holy, and the commandment holy, and righteous, and good" (Romans 7:7-12).

Walking in the Light

"Did then that which is good become death to me? May it never be! But sin, that it might be shown to be sin, was producing death in me through that which is good; that through the commandment sin might become exceedingly sinful. For we know that the law is spiritual, but I am fleshly, sold under sin" (Romans 7:13-14).

To paraphrase, Paul is explaining to the brothers, "Did the law cause my death? Absolutely not! The law is good. The law is spiritual. However, as long as I am under the law, sin is empowered to produce in me every manner of sin, every manner of evil, resulting in death. As a person that has not experienced being baptized into Christ's death, as a person that has not experienced being raised up with Christ through the power of His resurrection, I am still fleshly, I am still carnal. I am still sold into sin's power."

Paul is explaining to the brothers his experience while he was still under the law, still enslaved to sin, so they would understand the importance of realizing themselves as dead to sin and no longer being controlled by it since being baptized by the Spirit into Christ's death. "For sin will not rule over you, because you are not under law but under grace" (Romans 6:14, NASB).

In Christ, we are freed, liberated from the dominion of sin because we are no longer enslaved to sin. The Son has set us free! Through our death with Christ, we have been liberated, freed from sin and the law!

We are set free through our baptism, by the Spirit, into the death and resurrection of Christ to walk in a new way of life. We are no longer obligated to walk according to the flesh. We are now set free to walk according to the leading and the empowerment of the indwelling Holy Spirit.

Paul continues in Romans 7:15-20 to describe to these brothers his experience while he was still under the law, still enslaved to sin, saying, "For that which I do, I do not approve of. And that which I don't want to do, I practice. For I even do things that I detest.

Jon von Ernst

"But if I practice these things and yet I don't agree with them, I consent that the law is good. So now it is no longer "I" who do it but the sinful nature which lives in me. Now I know that in me, that is in my flesh, lives a nature which is not good.

"For the willingness is present with me, but actually doing that which is good is not. And the good that I want to do, I don't do. But the evil which I don't want to do, I practice. But if I practice that which I don't want to do, it is no longer "I" who do it but the sinful nature which lives in me." (Romans 7:15-20, TFLV).

This is in direct contrast to the Christian life lived in obedience to the leading of the indwelling Holy Spirit. A genuine Spirit filled Christian is led by the Spirit and empowered by that Spirit to be able to hear and obey that leading.

The born-again Christian is no longer enslaved by sin, he is no longer forced to do sin's will. He has been set free to walk in newness of life enslaved to righteousness and obedient to God's leading through the Holy Spirit. Therefore, Paul exclaims in Philippians 4:13, "I can do all things through Christ who strengthens me!"

Paul is illustrating that the person that is still under the law is still in bondage to sin. They do not have the ability to do the good that they want to do because they do not have the Spirit of Christ within them empowering them to do it. They are not spiritual. They are merely natural men.

They agree with the law that it is good, but they have no ability to do the good that they desire to do. The person under the law, in bondage to sin, eventually ends up practicing the evil that he does not want to do. Evil and sin become a way of life to him.

Paul exposes this way of life in his letter to the believers in the churches of Galatia. "Now the deeds of the flesh are evident, which are: sexual immorality, impurity, indecent behavior, idolatry, witchcraft, hostilities, strife, jealousy, outbursts of anger, selfish ambition, dissensions, factions, envy, drunkenness, carousing, and things like these, of which

Walking in the Light

I forewarn you, just as I have forewarned you, that those who practice such things will not inherit the kingdom of God" (Galatians 5:19-21, HCSB).

Paul could not be more clear. Those who practice the works of the flesh will not inherit the kingdom of God. Those who practice evil will not inherit the kingdom of God! Genuine Christians are led and empowered by the indwelling Holy Spirit to live holy lives, to live just as Jesus lived.

John concurs,"By this we know that we have come to know Him, if we keep His commandments. The one who says, "I have come to know Him," and does not keep His commandments, is a liar, and the truth is not in him; but whoever follows His word, in him the love of God has truly been perfected. By this we know that we are in Him: the one who says that he remains in Him ought, himself also, walk just as He walked" (1 John 2:3-6, NASB).

Paul continues, explaining to the brothers the wretched predicament of the person that is under the law and delights in the law in his mind. This person finds himself in a war, a war that he, in his own strength, cannot possibly win.

"I delight in God's law after the inward person, but I see a different law in my members, warring against the law of my mind, and bringing me into captivity under the law of sin which is in my members. What a wretched man I am! Who will deliver me out of the body of this death? I thank God through Jesus Christ, our Lord! So then with the mind, I myself serve God's law, but with the flesh, sin's law" (Romans 7:22-25).

The unsaved person that is under the law delights in the law of God and desires to do the good that it requires. However, he has no ability to do that good because there is a different law in his flesh that is warring against the law in his mind. The law in his flesh is bringing him into captivity under the law of sin.

What a dreadful state he finds himself in. Eventually, in total despair, this unsaved man cries out to God to be delivered from this body of death. Finally, he finds deliverance through

Christ Jesus our Lord and makes the proclamation we find in the beginning of Romans chapter eight.

"The law of the Spirit of life in Christ Jesus made me free from the law of sin and of death." The condemnation of slavery to sin has been removed through his baptism into Christ's death by faith in Jesus.

He is now, as a born-again, Spirit filled believer, set free from slavery to sin. He is now empowered by the indwelling Holy Spirit to do all the good that God commands him to do. He is no longer forced, by the sin in his flesh, to practice the evil that he hates. He is no longer a wretched, merely human man, but he is now a spiritual man empowered by the indwelling Holy Spirit to live a holy, godly life.

Chapter 5 Discussion Questions:
A Wretched Man

1. Who sinned resulting in sin entering the world and death passing unto all men?
2. When Adam sinned, how was his nature changed?
3. What truth was the basis for God's condemnation passed against Adam for his sin?
4. What frees us from this condemnation?
5. Should we continue to sin?
6. When we were baptized by the Holy Spirit into Christ, what were we baptized into?
7. Why was the old self crucified?
8. By His death we are dead to sin, by what power are we made alive to God?
9. In chapter seven, Paul is speaking to brothers that know the law, what is he stressing to them?
10. Why have we been discharged from the law?
11. Why must we know our death with Christ?
12. What is our death to sin based on?
13. What does the law expose?

Walking in the Light

14. Why is a person still fleshly, still sold under sin's power?
15. Why does the merely natural man, still under the law, not have the ability to do the good they want to do?
16. Who will inherit the kingdom of God?
17. According to 1 John 2:3-6, who is a liar?
18. What sets us free from the law of sin and of death?
19. Why is a born-again, Spirit-filled man no longer a wretched merely human man?

Chapter 6

Escaping the Devil's Trap

According to Paul, the unsaved person that is under the law and delights in the law of God, desires to do the good that it requires. However, because he is not spiritual, he does not have the indwelling Holy Spirit to empower him to do the good he desires to do. He has no ability to do that good because there is a different law in his flesh that is warring against the law in his mind. The law in his flesh is bringing him into captivity under the law of sin and of death.

In Romans 7:13-24, Paul describes the experience of the unsaved person that is under the law and delights in the law of God saying, "I am unspiritual, sold as a slave to sin" (7:14, NIV). "The desire to do what is good is with me, but there is no ability to do it" (7:18, HCSB). "The good that I want, I do not do, but I practice the very evil that I do not want" (7:19, NASB). "I see another law in my members, warring against the law of my mind, and bringing me into captivity to the law of sin which is in my members" (7:23, KJV).

What a dreadful state this merely natural, unsaved person finds himself in. Eventually, in total despair, he cries out to God to be delivered from this body of death. Finally, he finds deliverance through Christ Jesus the Lord and as a born-again, spiritual man, makes the proclamation we find in the beginning of Romans chapter eight.

"There is therefore now no condemnation to those who are in Christ Jesus, who don't walk according to the flesh, but according to the Spirit. For the law of the Spirit of life in Christ

Jesus made me free from the law of sin and of death" (Romans 8:1-2).

By faith in Christ, the law of the Spirit of life in Christ Jesus has now set him free from the law of sin and of death. The condemnation of slavery to sin has been removed through his baptism into Christ's death by faith in Jesus. Having been baptized, by the Spirit, into Christ's death, the believer is now made alive unto God, by that selfsame Spirit, to walk in a new way of life.

Having become a Christian, a spiritual man, by being born again, he is no longer a slave to sin, but now is a slave to righteousness, a slave to God. He is now empowered by the Spirit to walk according to the leading of the Spirit. He is no longer enslaved to sin and forced to walk according to the flesh. He now is able to walk according to the Spirit, doing the good that God commands him to do.

"Therefore there is now no condemnation at all for those who are in Christ Jesus. For the law of the Spirit of life in Christ Jesus has set you free from the law of sin and of death. For what the Law could not do, weak as it was through the flesh, God did: sending His own Son in the likeness of sinful flesh and as an offering for sin, He condemned sin in the flesh, so that the requirement of the Law might be fulfilled in us who do not walk according to the flesh but according to the Spirit." (Romans 8:1-4, NASB).

Now, here is the main point that I want to make concerning Romans chapter seven. Paul's account in Romans 7:13-24 describes his experience while under the law before being saved and becoming a Christian. In this passage he says he is "unspiritual, sold as a slave to sin."

He says he desires to do good, "but there is no ability to do it." Because he is a merely natural man, he does not have the Holy Spirit dwelling in him to set him free from bondage to sin and enable him to do the good that he wants to do.

He says he does not do the good he wants, "but I practice the very evil that I do not want." He says the law of sin in his flesh is "warring against the law of my mind, and bringing me into captivity to the law of sin which is in my members."

However, many professing Christians believe Paul is speaking in this passage about his experience after he became a Christian. They believe this because that is what they have been taught. They also believe it because it describes their own experience since becoming a Christian.

If you have not been born again, your experience as a professing Christian will be exactly as Paul describes in Romans 7:13-24. Without having been baptized into Christ's death we cannot walk in a new way of life. Without the empowering of the indwelling Holy Spirit, you are still enslaved to sin, and you do not have the ability to live a holy life.

There are few things in life more pitiful than a person attempting to live the Christian life without the Spirit of Christ living in them, teaching them, comforting them, and empowering them to walk in obedience to God. The Spirit of Christ within the believer empowers him to live a life of obedience. The Spirit of Christ enables the believer to live a holy life, to walk as Jesus walked.

Jesus declares, "I assure you: Unless someone is born of water and the Spirit, he cannot enter the kingdom of God. Whatever is born of the flesh is flesh, and whatever is born of the Spirit is spirit" (John 3:5-6, HCSB). You must be born again. You must be born of the Spirit!

The merely natural man cannot please God. Without the Spirit of Christ in Him, the merely natural man has no ability to do the good that he wants to do. Only the spiritual man, the person that has been born again, born from above, is empowered by the indwelling Spirit of Christ to do everything that God in Christ commands him to do.

The believer that has been born of the Spirit not only is forgiven of his past sins, he is also set free, through his death with Christ, from bondage to sin. Sin no longer has dominion over him. It is only when we have come to know our death with Christ that we can experience being dead to sin and being liberated from its dominion over us. We must know our death with Christ so we may truly consider ourselves dead to sin!

There are some that teach that in Romans chapter seven, Paul is describing his own experience as a spirit filled, born-again believer. They look at the passage in Romans 7:13-24 and say, "See, I am not so bad. I have the same problem Paul did after he got saved. Paul's Christian life was a continual struggle with sin in his flesh."

They use this teaching to justify themselves being enslaved to sin even though they claim to be Christians. This gives them, and those that hear this teaching, a false sense of peace with God. They comfort themselves with the thought that the sinful life they are living is just like Paul's. They have been badly deceived, not understanding the scriptures nor the power of God (Mark 12:24).

Not understanding scripture, they have failed to realize the main point that Paul is making in this whole section of Romans from the middle of chapter five through the end of chapter eight. They have failed to realize that the Son has set us free from the law of sin and of death through the Sprit of life in Christ Jesus that every true believer has been baptized into. Having been crucified with Christ through baptism into His death, the true believer has died to sin.

As genuine Christians, sin no longer has dominion over us! We have been set free from slavery to sin by the power of Christ's resurrection through the indwelling Holy Spirit. This indwelling Holy Spirit is the power of God which is working mightily in us who have truly trusted in Christ. It is empowering us to live holy lives that are pleasing to God.

These false teachers cannot understand or even relate to the idea of being able to live a holy life, because they have never experienced the power of God enabling them to do so. They have a form of godliness, but deny the power thereof. They deny that this indwelling Holy Spirit has set us free and is empowering the true believer to live holy lives, because they themselves have never experienced it. It is foolishness to them.

Jon von Ernst

The very idea of someone being able to live a holy life is offensive to them.

It is incredibly dangerous for the merely natural man, that neither understands the scriptures nor the power of God, to be teaching anyone else about the things of God. Paul explains, "A natural person does not accept the things of the Spirit of God, for they are foolishness to him; and he cannot understand them, because they are spiritually discerned" (1 Corinthians 2:14). This is a perfect example of the blind leading the blind. They will both fall into the pit.

If Paul's account in Romans 7:13-24 was a description of his life after being saved, then Paul must have been the biggest hypocrite that ever lived. If he was continually living in sin while teaching and exhorting everyone else that they must put off the old man and put on Christ, living lives worthy of the kingdom, he must have been the greatest deceiver, the greatest hypocrite of all time.

Can anyone that has read Paul's writings believe that his life was a continual struggle with sin? Could Paul's Christian experience have been that of a carnal believer, sold into bondage to sin (Romans 7:14)? Is it possible that Paul, being indwelt by the Holy Spirit, had no ability to do the good that he wanted to do (Romans 7:18)? Is it possible that Paul, as a Christian, practiced the evil that he hated (Romans 7:19)? If that was truly Paul's Christian experience, then his writings are total hypocrisy.

To understand scripture properly, it is important to look at the context in which the passage you are considering appears. We have been looking at the immediate context in which chapter seven of Romans appears. We have been looking at the section of Romans from the middle of chapter five to the end of chapter eight.

Now, we need to expand our view and look at chapter seven in the context of the entire book of Romans. Is the idea that Paul was speaking in Romans 7:13-24 of his experience as a born-again, Spirit-filled believer consistent with what he wrote in the rest of the book of Romans?

Walking in the Light

Let us review some of the things that Paul wrote throughout the rest of this same book of Romans. "Paul, a slave of Christ Jesus, called as an apostle and singled out for God's good news— which He promised long ago through His prophets in the Holy Scriptures— concerning His Son, Jesus Christ our Lord, who was a descendant of David according to the flesh and who has been declared to be the powerful Son of God by the resurrection from the dead according to the Spirit of holiness. We have received grace and apostleship through Him to bring about the obedience of faith among all the nations on behalf of His name (Romans 1:1-5, HCSB).

Paul says in this passage that he is a slave of Jesus Christ. He says he has received grace to bring about obedience. He seems to understand his mission in the Spirit and that he has received everything required to complete it. "For God is my witness, whom I serve in my spirit in the Good News of his Son" (Romans 1:9).

"For the wrath of God is revealed from heaven against all ungodliness and unrighteousness of men who suppress the truth in unrighteousness" (Romans 1:18). Paul clearly understands God's displeasure with all ungodliness and unrighteousness.

"Even as they refused to have God in their knowledge, God gave them up to a reprobate mind, to do those things which are not fitting; being filled with all unrighteousness, sexual immorality, wickedness, covetousness, malice; full of envy, murder, strife, deceit, evil habits, secret slanderers, backbiters, hateful to God, insolent, arrogant, boastful, inventors of evil things, disobedient to parents, without understanding, covenant breakers, without natural affection, unforgiving, unmerciful; who, knowing the ordinance of God, that those who practice such things are worthy of death, not only do the same, but also approve of those who practice them" (Romans 1:28-32).

Knowing this, how could Paul live his Christian life practicing the evil that he hated? God "will pay back to everyone according to their works: to those who by perseverance in well-doing seek for glory, honor, and incorruptibility, eternal life; but to those who are self-seeking, and don't obey the truth, but obey unrighteousness, will be wrath, indignation, oppression, and anguish on every soul of man who does evil, to the Jew first, and also to the Greek" (Romans 2:6-9).

"As many as have sinned under the law will be judged by the law. For it isn't the hearers of the law who are righteous before God, but the doers of the law will be justified" (Romans 2:12-13). These verses demonstrate God's displeasure with the life style described in Romans 7:13-24. That life style is not acceptable for a heathen, much less for a Christian.

"Indeed you bear the name of a Jew, rest on the law, glory in God, know his will, and approve the things that are excellent, being instructed out of the law, and are confident that you yourself are a guide of the blind, a light to those who are in darkness, a corrector of the foolish, a teacher of babies, having in the law the form of knowledge and of the truth.

"You therefore who teach another, don't you teach yourself? You who preach that a man shouldn't steal, do you steal? You who say a man shouldn't commit adultery, do you commit adultery? You who abhor idols, do you rob temples? You who glory in the law, do you dishonor God by disobeying the law? For 'the name of God is blasphemed among the Gentiles because of you'" (Romans 2:17-24).

"If any man doesn't have the Spirit of Christ, he is not his. If Christ is in you, the body is dead because of sin, but the spirit is alive because of righteousness. But if the Spirit of him who raised up Jesus from the dead dwells in you, he who raised up Christ Jesus from the dead will also give life to your mortal bodies through his Spirit who dwells in you.

"So then, brothers, we are debtors, not to the flesh, to live after the flesh. For if you live after the flesh, you must die; but if by the Spirit you put to death the deeds of the body, you will live. For as many as are led by the Spirit of God, these are children of God. For you didn't receive the spirit of bondage again to fear, but you received the Spirit of adoption, by whom we cry, 'Abba! Father!'" (Romans 8:9-15).

"If the first fruit is holy, so is the lump. If the root is holy, so are the branches. But if some of the branches were broken off, and you, being a wild olive, were grafted in among them and became partaker with them of the root and of the richness of the olive tree, don't boast over the branches. But if you boast, it is not you who support the root, but the root supports you. You will say then, 'Branches were broken off, that I might be grafted in.' True; by their unbelief they were broken off, and you stand by your faith.

"Don't be conceited, but fear; for if God didn't spare the natural branches, neither will he spare you. See then the goodness and severity of God. Toward those who fell, severity; but toward you, goodness, if you continue in his goodness; otherwise you also will be cut off" (Romans 11:16-22).

We stand by faith. If we do not continue by faith in the goodness of God, we also will be cut off. Are you walking by faith, trusting in the power of God to enable you to live a holy life pleasing to Him? Are you being led by the Spirit of God? Are you walking in obedience to His leading? Is the Spirit of Christ empowering you to live a Godly life? This is what Paul continually urged the believers to do.

"Therefore I urge you, brothers, by the mercies of God, to present your bodies a living sacrifice, holy, acceptable to God, which is your spiritual service. Don't be conformed to this world, but be transformed by the renewing of your mind, so that you may prove what is the good, well-pleasing, and perfect will of God" (Romans 12:1-2).

"Let love be without hypocrisy. Abhor that which is evil. Cling to that which is good" (Romans 12:9).

"Do this, knowing the time, that it is already time for you to awaken out of sleep, for salvation is now nearer to us than when we first believed. The night is far gone, and the day is near. Let's therefore throw off the deeds of darkness, and let's put on the armor of light. Let's walk properly, as in the day;

not in reveling and drunkenness, not in sexual promiscuity and lustful acts, and not in strife and jealousy. But put on the Lord Jesus Christ, and make no provision for the flesh, for its lusts" (Romans 13:11-14).

How do these passages match up with the idea that Paul was describing his experience as a Christian in Romans 7:13-24 where he speaks of having no ability to do the good that he wants to do, but practicing the evil that he hates? If Paul in Romans 7:13-24 is speaking of his experience as a Christian, how could he state in 2 Timothy 1:3, "I thank God, whom I serve with a clear conscience."

Paul describes in 1 Thessalonians 2:9-12 how he served God with a clear conscience. "For you remember, brothers, our labor and travail; for working night and day, that we might not burden any of you, we preached to you the Good News of God. You are witnesses with God how holy, righteously, and blamelessly we behaved ourselves toward you who believe. As you know, we exhorted, comforted, and implored every one of you, as a father does his own children, to the end that you should walk worthily of God, who calls you into his own Kingdom and glory."

It is hard to imagine how anyone could arrive at a more twisted view of scripture than to think that Romans 7:13-24 is Paul's description of his life as a Christian. Why would someone proclaim such an obviously false teaching? I believe one reason is that they either have never known the freedom that the genuine believer has in Christ Jesus as Lord or that they have known Him and have turned back and become entangled again in bondage to sin and are defeated.

Peter warns us, "There will be false teachers among you. They will secretly bring in destructive heresies, even denying the Master who bought them, and will bring swift destruction on themselves. Many will follow their unrestrained ways, and the way of truth will be blasphemed because of them. They will exploit you in their greed with deceptive words" (2 Peter 2:1-3).

Walking in the Light

He continues his warning, "These people are springs without water, mists driven by a whirlwind. The gloom of darkness has been reserved for them. For by uttering boastful, empty words, they seduce, with fleshly desires and debauchery, people who have barely escaped from those who live in error. They promise them freedom, but they themselves are slaves of corruption, since people are enslaved to whatever defeats them.

"For if, having escaped the world's impurity through the knowledge of our Lord and Savior Jesus Christ, they are again entangled in these things and defeated, the last state is worse for them than the first. For it would have been better for them not to have known the way of righteousness than, after knowing it, to turn back from the holy command delivered to them" (2 Peter 2:17-19).

I believe some of these people peddle these false teachings about Romans 7 to sooth their own conscience and to lead astray as many as possible to follow them. Jude explains, "For certain people have crept in unnoticed, those who were long beforehand marked out for this condemnation, ungodly persons who turn the grace of our God into indecent behavior and deny our only Master and Lord, Jesus Christ.

"These people are discontented grumblers, walking according to their desires; their mouths utter arrogant words, flattering people for their own advantage. But you, dear friends, remember what was predicted by the apostles of our Lord Jesus Christ; they told you, 'In the end time there will be scoffers walking according to their own ungodly desires.' These people create divisions and are merely natural, not having the Spirit" (Jude 1:4,16-19).

However, there may be some that teach these lies out of ignorance, never having been taught by the Spirit, but only taught by men, who were taught by men, who were taught by men. They may have believed what they heard from another false teacher and never searched the scriptures or sought the leading of the Holy Spirit for understanding.

This false teaching of Romans seven is extremely harmful to Christians and to those that profess to be Christians. These lies wink at sin. They treat sin as though it is not serious. They even treat sin as the expected, constant, everyday experience of the Christian.

Do you have the Spirit of Christ? Have you been enabled by the Spirit of Christ to live in obedience to the leading of the indwelling Holy Spirit? What fruit is being produced in your life. The scriptures tell us that we can know a tree by the fruit it bears. Does your claim to be a Christian agree with the fruit that is being produced in your life?

This false teaching regarding Paul's testimony in Romans 7:13-24 robs the professing Christian of the realization that they need to be born of the Spirit. It prevents them from realizing that they need the Holy Spirit to come and live in them and empower them to live godly, holy lives. It robs them of the understanding presented throughout the Bible that God expects His people to live holy lives. It also robs them of the understanding that God will severely punish those that do not.

When we are living in sin God is not pleased with us. When we sin, we must immediately repent as soon as we become aware of the sin, and humbly turn back to God. We, as Christians, should never accept any excuse for sin in our lives. We have been given, in the indwelling Holy Spirit, everything required for life and godliness (2 Peter 1:3). We are without excuse!

If you have spread false teachings, do not despair. You can purify yourself by repenting, turning away from the false teachings and turning back to God and to the truth as it is in Jesus.

Paul writes to us in 2 Timothy 2:14-26, telling us about false teachers who had deviated from the truth, whose word spread like a gangrene overturning the faith of some. He says if anyone purifies himself from these false teachings, he will be a special instrument, set apart and prepared for every good work. He tells us to instruct our "opponents with gentleness. Perhaps God will grant them repentance to know the truth.

Then they may come to their senses and escape the Devil's trap, having been captured by him to do his will."

It is my prayer that those that read this brief message will purify themselves from these false teachings and escape the Devil's trap by returning to the truth and living according to it. "The Lord knows those who are His, and everyone who names the name of the Lord must turn away from unrighteousness" (2 Timothy 2:19).

Chapter 6 Discussion Questions:
Escaping the Devil's Trap

1. How is the condemnation of slavery to sin removed?
2. How is the believer made alive unto God?
3. In whom is the requirement of the law fulfilled?
4. There are few things in life more pitiful than what?
5. What do some use Romans 7 to justify?
6. What is this power of God that works in the believer?
7. What does it mean to have a form of religion, but to deny the power thereof?
8. What do those that live according to the Spirit set their minds on?
9. Who belongs to Christ?
10. Who will be cut off if they do not continue in God's goodness?
11. How is the believer transformed?
12. When we put on the Lord Jesus Christ, what are we to make no provision for?
13. For whom is their last state worse than the first?
14. What do these false teachings rob the Christians of?
15. Why are Christians without excuse when they sin?
16. How can we purify ourselves of these false teachings?

Chapter 7

That He Might Have Mercy On All

Words are important. It is through the use of words that we communicate with one another. However, to be able to communicate effectively, all parties involved must share a common understanding of the meaning intended by each of the words used in our communication. If I use a word intending to mean one thing, and you hear that word and understand it to mean something totally different, we end up talking in circles, with neither party understanding what the other is trying to communicate.

This often happens when we discuss the scriptures and the spiritual concepts presented in the scriptures. We often have an understanding of the meaning of the words used in scripture that differs completely from what the person that originally wrote that portion of the scriptures, being led by the Holy Spirit, intended those words to mean. When we do this, we develop a theology, based on our misunderstanding of that passage of scripture, that is in total contrast to what the writer of the scripture ever intended.

To avoid this, sometimes tragic mistake, we must take great pains to ensure that our understanding of the intended meaning of the words used in the scriptures is correctly discerned. To do this, it is important, whenever we approach any passage of scripture, to leave all of our preconceptions that we may have picked up, from study bibles, commentaries, and various writers and speakers, at the door. We must come before God prayerfully, with an open mind, prepared to listen as He speaks to us, by His Spirit, through the passage of scripture before us.

When we encounter a word in our English translation of the Bible whose meaning may be unclear, we might consult a concordance to gain more understanding of what meaning was originally intended. The concordance will tell us which word in the original Greek or Hebrew language was translated into the particular English word in question. We will then able to review the various meanings of the word used in the original Greek or Hebrew, and based on the context in which they are used, receive a better understanding of what the writer of the passage originally intended the word to mean.

We may then be led by the Spirit to consider other similar passages in scripture that may enhance our understanding of the meaning intended to be communicated by the use of the word in question. We do this to get a broader understanding of the context within which the word is used. As we do this, we allow the scriptures to interpret the scriptures.

When allowing the scriptures to interpret the scriptures, it is not unusual to find that you come away with a totally different understanding of the subject matter covered in that passage of scripture than you had ever considered before. An even greater blessing is when you begin to realize that this new understanding begins to open your eyes to a lot of other areas of scripture that may have seemed difficult to understand, perhaps to passages of scripture that seemed to contradict each other. Now, however, these, and so many other passages, suddenly all seem to fit together and you rejoice in how God is revealing so much more of Himself and His ways to you.

This is exactly what we want to do right now. We are going to look at some passages of scripture and seek enlightenment from the Lord to enable us to understand the meaning He intended to communicate to us by the use of some very specific words whose meanings have often been confused and interchanged.

We will begin by considering God's plan to make salvation and the forgiveness of sins available to the entire world and the words He used to describe this plan. We will begin by turning to Romans chapter eleven.

Paul writes to believers in Rome, "As you once disobeyed God, but now have received mercy through their disobedience, so they too have now disobeyed, resulting in mercy to you, so that they also now may receive mercy. For God has imprisoned all in disobedience, so that He may have mercy on all" (Romans 11:30-32, HCSB).

Now here is a word that deserves some consideration as to what the writer intended it to mean. What exactly is meant by the Greek word 'eleos' that is translated as mercy. God has imprisoned all in disobedience that He might have mercy on all.

Mercy is defined as compassion or forgiveness shown toward someone that is within one's power to punish or harm. Paul, writing in Romans 6:23, tells us, "For the wages of sin is death." Under God's righteousness, man, by virtue of his sin and rebellion against God and His authority, has incurred a debt that he will never be able to repay except by the forfeiture of his own life.

However, God, because of His mercy and love, has compassion on us and sends His only Son to die in our place, paying our debt in full. God's mercy is demonstrated, because of His love, by His willingness to release us from an insurmountable debt. This is God's mercy, His compassion. It is unmerited, yet it is freely available to all who, by faith, will simply receive it by believing in Jesus.

Paul continues to explain in Romans 5:8, "God commends his own love toward us, in that while we were yet sinners, Christ died for us." While we were still sinners, unable to pay God the huge debt that we had incurred through our disobedience, God had mercy on us. While we were without any merit, He demonstrated His love for us by sending His only Son to pay the full price of our debt. Christ fully paid our debt by freely giving His life to die in our place, in our behalf.

It was within God's power to require our death as payment for our disobedience, our sin. Yet, by His incredible mercy and

Walking in the Light

love, He had compassion on us, while we were yet sinners, while we were yet totally undeserving, totally helpless. This was a completely unmerited display of God's love and of God's mercy.

Paul expresses this very clearly in his letter to the church in Ephesus. "But God, being rich in mercy because of his great love with which he loved us, even when we were "dead" because of our sins, gave us his own life together with the Anointed One" (Ephesians 2:4-5, TFLV).

Again, Paul writes to Titus reminding him about God's compassion. "But when the kindness of God our Savior and his love toward mankind appeared, not by works of righteousness which we did ourselves, but according to his mercy, he saved us through the washing of regeneration and renewing by the Holy Spirit" (Titus 3:4-5).

What a demonstration of God's love this was! It was not because of any righteousness on our part. It was totally according to His mercy. This plan of God, to demonstrate His kindness and love toward us while we were helpless and undeserving, was formulated long before the earth was even formed.

"Knowing that you were not redeemed with perishable things like silver or gold from your futile way of life inherited from your forefathers, but with precious blood, as of a lamb unblemished and spotless, the blood of Christ. For He was foreknown before the foundation of the world, but has appeared in these last times for the sake of you who through Him are believers in God, who raised Him from the dead and gave Him glory, so that your faith and hope are in God" (1 Peter 1:18-21).

Before the foundation of the earth had even been laid, God knew that the man He would form from the dust of the ground would sin by disobeying His command and rebelling against His authority. He knew that He would need to have a spotless lamb prepared to offer up to redeem man back to Himself. Once redeemed and made holy by the blood of this spotless lamb, Jesus Christ our Lord, man could be reconciled to God, beginning the process of full salvation.

When He created man, God prepared man for this process by forming man in a very special way. God gave man a free will. He gave man the ability to think and to choose who he would obey and consequently, how he would live.

God also gave man another very special gift. God has apportioned to each person a measure of faith. Everyone exercises this gift, their measure of faith, to believe in something. Some believe in themselves, in their righteousness, in their strength, intellect, or natural abilities. Some believe in other people. Some believe in superstitions and false gods. Still others have chosen to believe in the one true living God and the One He sent, Jesus Christ our Lord.

God gave each person a free will and a measure of faith. He gave man the ability to think, to consider what is true and what he would choose to believe in by exercising this portion of faith that was allotted to him.

Paul reveals this truth to us in Romans 12:3, "For I say through the grace that was given me, to every man who is among you, not to think of himself more highly than he ought to think; but to think reasonably, as God has apportioned to each person a measure of faith."

Man now had everything he needed to be able to receive God's wonderful gift of love and mercy that He was about to make freely available to every person in the world. God was simply waiting for just the right moment. "At just the right time, when we were still powerless, Christ died for the ungodly" (Romans 5:6, NIV).

All that God requires now is that we, individually, respond to the good news about this gift of mercy and choose to receive it. We receive it by exercising the portion of faith that He has allotted to each one of us. We exercise this portion of faith by choosing to believe in the One He has sent.

When we exercise our portion of faith, we join our faith together with works of obedience in order to receive this free gift. One of these works of obedience is believing.

Walking in the Light

Jesus tells us in John 6:26-29, "Most certainly I tell you, you seek me, not because you saw signs, but because you ate of the loaves, and were filled. Don't work for the food which perishes, but for the food which remains to eternal life, which the Son of Man will give to you. For God the Father has sealed him.

"They said therefore to him, 'What must we do, that we may work the works of God?' Jesus answered them, 'This is the work of God, that you believe in him whom he has sent.'" Believing is the work that God requires in response to the good news of Jesus dying in our place, paying the full price for our sins and redeeming us back to God.

God, in His righteousness, can require works on our part to receive His free gift of salvation and the forgiveness of sins because even the faith that we must exercise is a gift from Him intended for this very purpose. We receive this free gift of salvation by listening to the good news presented by God through the scriptures and through the testimony of other believers, even through the testimony of creation itself, weighing the evidence presented, and choosing whether we will believe or not believe.

The one that believes is greatly rewarded and benefits richly from all that Christ has done on our behalf. Those that choose not to believe receive no benefit and remain under condemnation.

"For God so loved the world, that He gave His only Son, so that everyone who believes in Him will not perish, but have eternal life. For God did not send the Son into the world to judge the world, but so that the world might be saved through Him.

"The one who believes in Him is not judged; the one who does not believe has been judged already, because he has not believed in the name of the only Son of God . . . The one who believes in the Son has eternal life; but the one who does not obey the Son will not see life, but the wrath of God remains on him." (John 3:16-18, 36; NASB).

This passage informs us that God desires that none would perish, but that everyone might have the opportunity to receive eternal life. It also informs us about the way in which He plans on bringing this about. The way He plans to accomplish this is through sending His only Son into the world to take away the sins of the world and thereby reconcile the world unto Himself (2 Corinthians 5:19).

James writes to us about Abraham saying, "You see that his faith and his actions were working together, and his faith was made complete by what he did. And the scripture was fulfilled that says, 'Abraham believed God, and it was credited to him as righteousness,' and he was called God's friend. You see that a person is considered righteous by what they do and not by faith alone" (James 2:22-24, NIV).

What work did Abraham do? He believed! He exercised his God given gift of faith and joined it to his work of believing. Abraham believed God, and it was credited to him as righteousness.

When we exercise our faith and join it to the work of believing, other works begin to be produced by God's Spirit working in and through us. One of these works is repentance.

"Therefore, having overlooked the times of ignorance, God now commands all people everywhere to repent, because He has set a day when He is going to judge the world in righteousness by the Man He has appointed. He has provided proof of this to everyone by raising Him from the dead" (Acts 17:30-31, HCSB).

We are told in Acts 2:36-38 and 40, "'Let all the house of Israel therefore know certainly that God has made him both Lord and Christ, this Jesus whom you crucified.' Now when they heard this, they were cut to the heart, and said to Peter and the rest of the apostles, 'Brothers, what shall we do?'

"Peter said to them, 'Repent, and be baptized, every one of you, in the name of Jesus Christ for the forgiveness of sins, and you will receive the gift of the Holy Spirit . . . With many other words he testified, and exhorted them, saying, "Save yourselves from this crooked generation!"'"

Walking in the Light

This repentance is essential to receiving God's free gift of mercy. Jesus declared in Mark 1:15, "The time is fulfilled, and God's Kingdom is at hand! Repent, and believe in the Good News." Jesus warned in Luke 13:3 and again in Luke 13:5, "Unless you repent, you will all perish." Paul announces in Acts 17:30 that God "commands that all people everywhere should repent."

As our faith is joined together with works of believing and repenting, we find still other works beginning to be produced through God's drawing us to His Son. Believing in our hearts that God raised Jesus from the dead, we find ourselves beginning to confess Jesus as Lord!

Paul explains this process in Romans 10:8-10, "The word of faith which we preach: that if you will confess with your mouth that Jesus is Lord, and believe in your heart that God raised him from the dead, you will be saved. For with the heart, one believes resulting in righteousness; and with the mouth confession is made resulting in salvation."

When we respond to the good news of God's mercy and love, His unmerited compassion toward the whole world, by exercising our faith, believing in the One He sent, we receive the benefit He intended. We are forgiven and we are made alive with Christ, reconciled to God.

Those that refuse to believe will experience none of the benefits that God has so freely provided in Christ Jesus our Lord. They will remain under judgment and the condemnation of slavery to sin.

Remember Romans 11:32. "God has imprisoned all in disobedience, so that He may have mercy on all." This is exactly what Jesus spoke of in Luke 4:18-19. When He entered the synagogue, He took the scroll and finding the place where it is written He read: "The Spirit of the Lord is on me, because he has anointed me to preach good news to the poor. He has sent me to heal the broken hearted, to proclaim release to the captives, recovering of sight to the blind, to deliver those who are crushed, and to proclaim the acceptable year of the Lord."

God has imprisoned every person in disobedience. However, God is rich in mercy for by His great love He has provided release to the captives. He has made this freedom available to everyone of us, if only we exercise our faith to believe in the One He has sent.

We, in Christ, are proclaiming this good news. We are proclaiming freedom to all who will listen and believe. This is the good news of God's unmerited mercy and love!

Chapter 7 Discussion Questions:
That He Might Have Mercy on All

1. Why is it important that all parties involved in any communication have a common understanding of the words being used?
2. What happens when we have an understanding of the meaning of words being used in scripture that differs completely from what was intended by the writer of the scripture passage in question?
3. How can we avoid misunderstanding a passage of scripture?
4. When might we consult a concordance?
5. How can a concordance help us understand the meaning of a word?
6. What should be allowed to interpret a passage of scripture?
7. Why has God imprisoned all in disobedience?
8. What is mercy?
9. What is God's compassion?
10. How did God commend His own love and mercy toward us?
11. When was God's plan to demonstrate His mercy and love toward us formulated?
12. How is man able to believe in anything?
13. What must we join together with our faith?

Walking in the Light

14. What is the work of God?
15. Who receives the benefits of all that Christ has done on our behalf?
16. What work did Abraham do?
17. What happens when we respond to the good news of God's mercy, His compassion?

Chapter 8

Grace

"God has apportioned to each person a measure of faith" (Romans 12:3). God has given a measure of faith to every person. It is a gift from God. Everyone exercises this gift, their measure of faith, to believe in something. Some believe in themselves, in their strength, intellect, or natural abilities. Some believe in superstitions and false gods. Some have chosen to believe in the one true living God and the One He sent, Jesus Christ our Lord.

Paul writes in Romans 11:32, "For God has imprisoned all in disobedience, so that He may have mercy on all." God has imprisoned all in disobedience because all have sinned, so that He may have mercy on all. And again, in Ephesians 2:4, "But God, being rich in mercy, because of His great love with which He loved us."

God's mercy is extended to all. Man's sin had separated him from God. So God extended His mercy to all by sending His Son into the world to take away the sins of the world.

John the Baptist sees Jesus coming toward him and testifies, "Look, the Lamb of God, who takes away the sin of the world!" (John 1:29, NIV). 1 John 2:2 says, "He Himself (Christ) is the propitiation for our sins, and not only for ours, but also for those of the whole world." By sending Jesus into the world to take away the sins of the world, God was extending His mercy to all. God made His mercy freely available to all who would willingly receive it.

Paul declares, "He saved us, not on the basis of deeds which we did in righteousness, but in accordance with His mercy" (Titus 3:5). Those that chose to receive God's unmerited gift of mercy believed in Jesus. "To the one who does not work, but believes on Him who declares the ungodly to be righteous, his faith is credited for righteousness" (Romans 4:5, HCSB).

Those that did not trust in their own works, but exercised their faith to believe God, received the benefit of God's merciful gift. They received the benefit of that gift of righteousness through faith. By faith in Christ, they had their sins forgiven and were reconciled to God.

By virtue of being reconciled to God by obeying God and believing in Jesus, they found favor in the sight of God. By believing, they merited God's favor. Therefore, God blessed them by causing His power to work in them, sanctifying them by the working of His Holy Spirit. He caused the Holy Spirit to indwell them and make their spirit alive, restoring them to fellowship with God.

Now having been reconciled to God, much more, they are being saved by His grace. Paul writes, "For by grace you are being saved through faith" (Ephesians 2:8, TFLV). Through exercising their faith to believe in Jesus, the believer is now in the process of being saved by grace. God gives this grace to those that have merited it by exercising their faith to believe in Jesus.

Now that we have obeyed the good news, the gospel of the kingdom, we begin to receive of the many blessings that God has prepared for us in Christ. Being reconciled to God, justified by the blood of Christ, having our sins forgiven by His love and mercy, God begins to pour out His grace richly upon those that have obeyed the gospel and joined works of obedience to their faith. It is by this grace that we are now being saved.

Paul encourages us, "Therefore accept one another, even as Christ also accepted you, to the glory of God. Now I say that Christ has been made a servant of the circumcision for the truth of God, that he might confirm the promises given to the fathers, and that the Gentiles might glorify God for his mercy

. . . Now may the God of hope fill you with all joy and peace in believing, that you may abound in hope, in the power of the Holy Spirit" (Romans 15:7-9, 13).

This is the much more that Paul speaks of in Romans 5:8-10. "God demonstrates His own love toward us, in that while we were still sinners, Christ died for us. Much more then, having now been justified by His blood, we shall be saved from the wrath of God through Him. For if while we were enemies we were reconciled to God through the death of His Son, much more, having been reconciled, we shall be saved by His life." (NASB).

Again Paul writes, "For by grace you are being saved through faith which is not your own but instead is a gift from God" (Ephesians 2:8, TFLV). We have been saved, being justified by the blood of Christ and, by it, reconciled to God. We are now in the process of being saved by Christ's life within us, by this amazing grace of God.

This grace is what God is using to save us now in this new and ongoing phase of the salvation process. It is by God's grace that we are being brought on to maturity in Christ and are being purified, sanctified, and enabled to live a godly life in the midst of this corrupt sinful world. We are, right now, in this life, enabled by the leading and empowering of the Holy Spirit to live as Jesus lived, to walk as Jesus walked, fully pleasing to the Father.

This, now, is where we need to exercise the portion of faith that God has given to each of us. As we believed God for our initial salvation, now we need to believe God for our sanctification. As we believed God for our being restored to fellowship with Him by the blood of Jesus, we now need to believe God for our being transformed into the likeness of His son by the life of Christ working mightily within us by the power of the indwelling Holy Spirit.

As we believed God to free us from the penalty of sin, we now need to believe God to free us from the power of sin. We need to exercise our portion faith to believe that the life of Christ indwelling us as the Holy Spirit in our spirit is able to

Walking in the Light

lead us, empowering us to walk in continual obedience, abiding in Christ, doing the will of the Father, and not fulfilling the lust of the flesh.

This indwelling Holy Spirit will teach us all that is ours in Christ. He will cause us to know the hope of glory that is ours. "Christ in you, the hope of glory" (Colossians 1:27). We begin to know Him and the power of His resurrection and the fellowship of His sufferings, being conformed to His death, that we might attain unto the best resurrection.

God favors the righteous. "The eyes of the Lord are upon the righteous" (Psalm 34:15). He watches over them. "The Lord knows how to deliver the godly out of temptation and to keep the unrighteous under punishment for the day of judgment" (2 Peter 2:9). He protects the righteous, but He punishes the wicked.

God punishes those that refuse to believe in the One He sent, those that refuse to repent and turn back to Him. God gives His grace to those that have exercised their faith to believe in Jesus. They are no longer condemned. He does not give His grace to those that refuse to believe. They are condemned already and remain condemned unless they turn back to God and believe in the One He sent.

John 3:18 tells us, "Anyone who believes in Him is not condemned, but anyone who does not believe is already condemned, because he has not believed in the name of the One and Only Son of God." The word condemned in this passage refers to the condemnation that God sentenced Adam to when He judged his sin and passed the sentence of condemnation against him that he would be enslaved to sin. In Adam, all sinned and therefore were under God's condemnation as slaves to sin.

God, however, gives grace to those that merit His favor by faith in Jesus. Those that exercise their faith to believe in Jesus are set free, liberated, from this slavery to sin. They are no longer enslaved to sin. They have been justified, rendered innocent, in order to serve God in newness of life in the Spirit. They have been justified by receiving God's merited favor.

"So that having been justified by His grace, we may become heirs with the hope of eternal life" (Titus 3:7, HCSB). We that believe have been justified by grace. We now have the hope of eternal life.

Peter warns, "Be on your guard, so that you are not led away by the error of lawless people and fall from your own stability. But grow in the grace and knowledge of our Lord and Savior Jesus Christ" (2 Peter 3:17-18). To receive this eternal life and the full inheritance that God has for us, we must allow this grace to grow in us and accomplish all that God desires, bringing us to maturity by transforming us into the image of Christ.

But what do the scriptures mean by this word grace? The idea of grace as used in scripture is very difficult to define. It seems to be a very abstract concept. It has many different meanings depending on the context within which it is used. These meanings, however, seem to be various shades of just one general idea.

This general idea is that grace is the effect produced in a believer's heart and life as a response to God favoring that individual with His person, His presence, and His power. The effect produced as a result of the power of God working in the believer's life is a great state of gladness that enables them to rejoice always. It causes them to be filled with the joy of the Lord.

The word grace in the New Testament is the English translation of the Greek word charis. It appears some 150 times in the New Testament. According to *Strong's Concordance*, it means grace, favor which causes joy, pleasure, gratification, thankfulness.

Charis comes from the Greek root word chairo. Chairo means to rejoice, to be glad. There are ten other Greek words that come from the root word chairo. I will briefly identify each and give a brief explanation of their meanings according to Strong's.

The next most frequently used derivative of chairo, used 60 times, is chara. It means joy, joyful, the state of great happiness or gladness. The next is eucharisteo used 39 times. It means give thanks to or to be thankful for something that makes you glad.

The next is charizomai. It is used 23 times. It means to grant to, to forgive, or to freely give that which produces joy. The next is charisma which appears 17 times. It has the meaning of favor bestowed, that which is freely given, a gift.

The next is eucharistia which appears 15 times. It means thanksgiving, thankfulness. Next is charin which appears 9 times. It means the reaction because of a favor or gift.

Next is synchairo which appears 7 times. It means to rejoice along with, rejoice together. Next is acharistos which appears 2 times. The 'a' at the beginning of the word means the negative or the opposite meaning of the original word. Therefore, acharistos means ungrateful, unthankful. The next is charitoo which appears twice with the meaning of to bestow favor on, to highly favor. Finally, eucharistos appears one time with the meaning of thankfulness for something done.

When the meanings and the usages of the Greek words related to the Greek word translated as grace are reviewed, the flavor of the word grace becomes clear. Grace is God's favor, granted to those that are pleasing in His sight, and the corresponding reaction of joy and rejoicing that that favor produces in the life of the recipient of His favor. This favor of God can be manifested in various ways.

In some contexts, grace is used as part of a greeting. For example, "Grace and peace from God the Father and the Lord Jesus Christ" (Romans 1:7 and 15 others). Paul used some form of this greeting at the beginning of every letter he wrote to churches and individuals in the New Testament. Peter and John also used grace in the same context. Here it seems to have the meaning of joy.

Sometimes it is very useful when trying to understand the author's intended meaning of a word to substitute the meaning that you think that it may have for the word in question. We can do this for the word 'grace.' We could try substituting 'joy' for the word 'grace'. For example, Romans 1:7 could be rephrased as, "Joy and peace from God the Father and the Lord Jesus Christ"."

This is similar to Romans 15:32, "Now may the God of hope fill you with all joy and peace in believing, that you may abound in hope, in the power of the Holy Spirit." The word joy seems to work quite well as a meaning of grace in this context.

In another context, grace is used in the closing of many of Paul's letters as a sort of benediction. For example, "The grace of our Lord Jesus Christ be with you" (Romans 16:24). Here grace seems to indicate something about an awareness of the presence of Christ in the believer's life that produces a deep sense of inner joy or enjoyment.

In other contexts, grace seems to have a different meaning. For example, "For by grace you are being saved through faith" (Ephesians 2:8, TFL). This passage reminds me of Paul writing to the believers in Rome "Much more then, since we have now been declared righteous by His blood, we will be saved through Him from wrath. For if, while we were enemies, we were reconciled to God through the death of His Son, then how much more, having been reconciled, will we be saved by His life!" (Romans 5:9-10, HCSB).

In Ephesians 2:8, grace is referring to something that is working within the born-again believer to save him. The genuine believer has already been saved by being born again, born from above. He has been saved by being reconciled to God by the death of God's Son, Jesus Christ.

However, having been saved by having been declared righteous by the blood of Christ that was shed for us, in fact, shed for the whole world, we will be saved through Him, through Christ Himself, from wrath. We will be saved by His life. The life of Christ, working within the believer after he has been born of the Spirit will, if the believer allows it by obeying its leading, save the believer from wrath.

In this context, grace is the enjoyment, the confidence, the courage, the strength, that is experienced by the believer in becoming aware of the reality of the person and power of

Walking in the Light

Christ working within him, by the indwelling Holy Spirit, both to know and to do the will of God. "But we have this treasure in clay vessels, that the exceeding greatness of the power may be of God, and not from ourselves (2 Corinthians 4:7).

In Acts chapter 3, after the lame man was healed, the crowd rushed over to Peter and John greatly wondering about the power that had healed him. Upon seeing them, Peter said to the people, "You men of Israel, why do you marvel at this man? Why do you fasten your eyes on us, as though by our own power or godliness we had made him walk?" Peter tried to assure the people that the power that healed the lame man was not of themselves, but it was the power of God operating through faith in the name of Jesus.

Paul writes to the church in Ephesus, "I pray that the eyes of your heart may be enlightened, so that you will know what is the hope of His calling, what are the riches of the glory of His inheritance in the saints, and what is the boundless greatness of His power toward us who believe. These are in accordance with the working of the strength of His might. . . I was made a minister, according to the gift of God's grace which was given to me according to the working of His power. . . Now to Him who is able to do far more abundantly beyond all that we ask or think, according to the power that works within us, to Him be the glory in the church and in Christ Jesus to all generations forever and ever. Amen" (Ephesians 1:18-19, 3:7, 20-21, NASB).

Paul was praying that God would open the eyes of the believers that they might know the boundless greatness of God's power working within them. The gift of God's grace was given to Paul according to the working of this power of God. God is able to do all we need through the working of His great power working within us. This indwelling Holy Spirit, the Spirit of the glorified Christ, is the power of God working within the believer to know and to do His will.

Let's look at the account of Stephen in the book of Acts. Stephen is testifying to the religious leaders of Israel. The scriptures describe Stephen during this encounter in Acts 6:8

and again in Acts 7:55, "Stephen, full of faith and power, performed great wonders and signs among the people... But Stephen, full of the Holy Spirit, looked up to heaven and saw the glory of God, and Jesus standing at the right hand of God."

Being full of the Holy Spirit, Stephen was full of faith and he was full of the power of God working in him. It was this power of God, not his own strength or natural ability, that enabled him to testify of the glory of God in Christ even while he was being stoned to death for his faith.

Paul explains, "For it is God who is at work in you, both to desire and to work for His good pleasure. . . For our citizenship is in heaven, from which we also eagerly wait for a Savior, the Lord Jesus Christ; who will transform the body of our lowly condition into conformity with His glorious body, by the exertion of the power that He has even to subject all things to Himself" (Philippians 2:13, 3:20-21, NASB).

Paul continues to explain the powerful working of Christ's strength, "God wanted to make known among the Gentiles the glorious wealth of this mystery, which is Christ in you, the hope of glory. We proclaim Him, warning and teaching everyone with all wisdom, so that we may present everyone mature in Christ. I labor for this, striving with His strength that works powerfully in me" (Colossians 1:27-29, HCSB).

The strength of Christ, working through the indwelling Holy Spirit, works powerfully in the believer to bring us to maturity and to conform us to His image. This is "Christ in you, the hope of glory."

As we attempt to understand the author's intended meaning of the word 'grace' let's try substituting 'the power of God' for the word 'grace'. For example, Ephesians 2:8 could be rephrased as, "For by the power of God you are being saved through faith." That sounds reasonable. Let's try this with some other verses where the word grace is used.

Romans 3:24 says, "They are justified freely by His grace through the redemption that is in Christ Jesus." That verse could be rephrased as, "They are justified freely by the power of God through the redemption that is in Christ Jesus." This is reminiscent of Romans 4:25, "He was delivered up for our trespasses and raised for our justification" and Philippians 3:10, "That I may know him, and the power of his resurrection." We are justified freely through the power of His resurrection.

Romans 4:16 says, "For this cause it is of faith, that it may be according to grace, to the end that the promise may be sure to all the offspring." This verse could be rephrased as, "For this cause it is of faith, that it may be according to the power of God, to the end that the promise may be sure to all the offspring."

Romans 5:17 says, "For if by the trespass of the one, death reigned through the one; so much more will those who receive the abundance of grace and of the gift of righteousness reign in life through the one, Jesus Christ." This verse could be rephrased as, "For if by the trespass of the one, death reigned through the one; so much more will those who receive the abundance of the power of God and of the gift of righteousness reign in life through the one, Jesus Christ."

1 Corinthians 1:4-5 says, "I always thank my God concerning you, for the grace of God which was given you in Christ Jesus; that in everything you were enriched in him, in all speech and all knowledge." This verse could be rephrased as, "I always thank God concerning you, for the power of God which was given you in Christ Jesus; that in everything you were enriched in him, in all speech and all knowledge."

As is becoming evident, this substitution could be done with a multitude of verses using the word grace in a similar context. The reading with this substitution seems quite reasonable. In a very real sense, grace is the power of God working in the life of the believer. However, there is more to the meaning of the word grace than just the power of God working in the life of the believer.

It is important to realize that the power of God working in the life of the believer produces a significant effect on the believer's heart and life. This effect on the believer's heart is very much related to the root word of grace, chairo. Chairo refers to being cheerful or calmly happy. It also refers to the meaning of charo, joy, joyful, the state of great happiness.

Nehemiah 8:10 reminds us, "Do not grieve, because your strength comes from rejoicing in the Lord." In John 15:11 Jesus says, "I have spoken these things to you so that My joy may be in you and your joy may be complete."

Paul writes in Philippians 4:4, "Rejoice in the Lord always! Again I will say, 'Rejoice!'" 1 Thessalonians 5:16-18 instructs us, "Always rejoice. Pray without ceasing. In everything give thanks, for this is the will of God in Christ Jesus toward you."

Joy and rejoicing is an essential element of this grace, this power of God working in us to transform us. This grace produces a joy and rejoicing in the Lord that works to change the very character of the believer.

God uses this joy produced by His power working within us to increase our desire for more of Him. He uses this joy to cause our love for Him to grow. God's grace utilizes the joy that it produces in our hearts to conform us to the image of Christ.

This transformation is accomplished by the believer continuing to joyfully walk by faith in obedience to the leading of the indwelling Holy Spirit. We are perfected, brought to maturity in Christ, not by our own effort, but by the grace of God working in us. If we allow it, this power of God working within us will enable us to endure to the end and inherit all that God has prepared for those that love Him and are the called according to His purpose.

Chapter 8 Discussion Questions:
Grace

1. To whom has God apportioned a measure of faith?
2. What is a gift that everyone has received from God?
3. What must a person do to believe in something?

4. Why has God imprisoned all in disobedience?
5. To whom did God's love and mercy extend?
6. How did God extend His mercy to all?
7. Whose sin is Christ the propitiation for?
8. On what basis did God save us?
9. What did those that chose to receive God's gift of mercy do?
10. Who received the benefit of God's merciful gift?
11. What benefit was received by those that exercised their faith to believe?
12. How does someone merit God's favor?
13. How does God favor those that believe in Jesus?
14. What is much more than being reconciled to God?
15. Who does God give His grace to?
16. Who does God protect and who does God punish?
17. What are we justified by?
18. Why must we be on guard?
19. What do the scriptures mean by the word grace?
20. What is grace?
21. In Ephesians 2:8, what word can we substitute for the word grace?
22. What is an essential element of this word grace, the power of God working in us to transform us?
23. How does God increase our desire for Himself?

Chapter 9

No Respecter of Persons

Grace is God's response to a person exercising their faith to believe God, to believe in the one that He has sent. Grace is also the reaction, in the believer's heart, to experiencing the power of God working in his life as a result of his faith being exercised to believe God and obey God. "We are his witnesses of these things; and so also is the Holy Spirit, whom God has given to those who obey him." (Acts 5:32).

Grace is God's favor poured out on the individual that believes God and obeys God. Grace is God's favor poured out on individuals that have merited it by faith, by believing God. This faith produces righteousness in the life of those that believe and obey God.

Noah found favor in the sight of the Lord. God favored Noah among all those of his generation because he was righteous. Genesis 6:5-9 says, "Then the LORD saw that the wickedness of mankind was great on the earth, and that every intent of the thoughts of their hearts was only evil continually. So the LORD was sorry that He had made mankind on the earth, and He was grieved in His heart.

"Then the LORD said, 'I will wipe out mankind whom I have created from the face of the land; mankind, and animals as well, and crawling things, and the birds of the sky. For I am sorry that I have made them.' But Noah found favor in the eyes of the LORD . . . Noah was a righteous man, blameless in his generation. Noah walked with God."

Hebrews 11:7 says, "By faith Noah, being warned by God about things not yet seen, in reverence prepared an ark for the salvation of his household, by which he condemned the world, and became an heir of the righteousness which is according to faith" (NASB).

Lot was favored by God and delivered from the judgment that God was bringing upon Sodom and Gomorrah because he was righteous. "Then the LORD said, 'The outcry against Sodom and Gomorrah is so great and their sin so grievous that I will go down and see if what they have done is as bad as the outcry that has reached me. If not, I will know.'

"The LORD said, 'If I find fifty righteous people in the city of Sodom, I will spare the whole place for their sake.' Then he (Abraham) said, 'May the Lord not be angry, but let me speak just once more. What if only ten can be found there?' He (the Lord) answered, 'For the sake of ten, I will not destroy it.' When the LORD had finished speaking with Abraham, he left, and Abraham returned home" (Genesis 18:21, 26, 32-33, NIV).

Peter reminds us, "For if God didn't spare the angels who sinned but threw them down into Tartarus and delivered them to be kept in chains of darkness until judgment; and if He didn't spare the ancient world, but protected Noah, a preacher of righteousness, and seven others, when He brought a flood on the world of the ungodly; and if He reduced the cities of Sodom and Gomorrah to ashes and condemned them to ruin, making them an example to those who were going to be ungodly; and if He rescued righteous Lot, distressed by the unrestrained behavior of the immoral (for as he lived among them, that righteous man tormented himself day by day with the lawless deeds he saw and heard)— then the Lord knows how to rescue the godly from trials and to keep the unrighteous under punishment until the day of judgment, especially those who follow the polluting desires of the flesh and despise authority" (2 Peter 2:4-10, HCSB).

The eyes of the Lord are upon the righteous to favor them with His protection. The Lord watches over His own. He protects them. He delivers them. However, God holds the sinful, those that continue to practice sin, those that live following the lustful desires of the flesh, for punishment on the day of judgment.

Abraham believed God and it was credited to him as righteousness. Here is a brief account of Abraham's journey of faith. "Now the LORD had said unto Abram, 'Get thee out of thy country, and from thy kindred, and from thy father's house, unto a land that I will shew thee: And I will make of thee a great nation, and I will bless thee, and make thy name great; and thou shalt be a blessing: And I will bless them that bless thee, and curse him that curseth thee: and in thee shall all families of the earth be blessed.' So Abram departed, as the LORD had spoken unto him; and Lot went with him: and Abram was seventy and five years old when he departed out of Haran" (Genesis 12:1-4, KJV).

"After these events, the word of the LORD came to Abram in a vision: 'Do not be afraid, Abram. I am your shield; your reward will be very great . . . one who comes from your own body will be your heir.' He took him outside and said, 'Look at the sky and count the stars, if you are able to count them.' Then He said to him, 'Your offspring will be that numerous.' Abraham believed the LORD; and He credited it to him as righteousness" (Genesis 15:1-6, HCSB).

"And when Abram was ninety years old and nine, the LORD appeared to Abram, and said unto him, I am the Almighty God; walk before me, and be thou perfect. And I will make my covenant between me and thee, and will multiply thee exceedingly. But my covenant will I establish with Isaac, which Sarah shall bear unto thee at this set time in the next year. And he left off talking with him, and God went up from Abraham" (Genesis 17:1-2, 20-21, KJV).

Finally, we read in Genesis chapter 22, "Now it came about after these things, that God tested Abraham, and said to him, 'Abraham!' And he said, 'Here I am.' Then He said, 'Take now your son, your only son, whom you love, Isaac, and go to the land of Moriah, and offer him there as a burnt offering on one of the mountains of which I will tell you.' So Abraham got up early in the morning and saddled his donkey, and took two of his young men with him and his son Isaac; and he split wood for the burnt offering, and set out and went to the place of which God had told him. On the third day Abraham raised his eyes and saw the place from a distance.

"Then Abraham said to his young men, 'Stay here with the donkey, and I and the boy will go over there; and we will worship and return to you.' And Abraham took the wood for the burnt offering and laid it on his son Isaac, and he took in his hand the fire and the knife. So the two of them walked on together. Isaac spoke to his father Abraham and said, 'My father!' And he said, 'Here I am, my son.' And he said, 'Look, the fire and the wood, but where is the lamb for the burnt offering?' Abraham said, 'God will provide for Himself the lamb for the burnt offering, my son.' So the two of them walked on together.

"Then they came to the place of which God had told him; and Abraham built the altar there and arranged the wood, and bound his son Isaac and laid him on the altar, on top of the wood. And Abraham reached out with his hand and took the knife to slaughter his son. But the angel of the LORD called to him from heaven and said, 'Abraham, Abraham!' And he said, 'Here I am.' He said, 'Do not reach out your hand against the boy, and do not do anything to him; for now I know that you fear God, since you have not withheld your son, your only son, from Me'" (Genesis 22:1-12, NASB).

Abraham believed God and it was credited to him as righteousness. Then God tested Abraham telling him to take His son Isaac up to the mountain and offer him up as a sacrifice to God. Abraham obeyed God. He took the most precious thing he had and proceeded to offer him up as he was commanded, until God stopped him. Abraham's obedience proved his faith in God.

We can say we believe, but does our obedience prove our belief is genuine? Do we actually obey God and do what He tells us to do?

Hebrews 11:8-12 says, "By faith, Abraham, when he was called, obeyed to go out to the place which he was to receive for an inheritance. He went out, not knowing where he went. By faith, he lived as an alien in the land of promise, as in a land not his own, dwelling in tents with Isaac and Jacob, the heirs with him of the same promise. For he looked for the city which has the foundations, whose builder and maker is God.

"By faith, even Sarah herself received power to conceive, and she bore a child when she was past age, since she counted him faithful who had promised. Therefore as many as the stars of the sky in multitude, and as innumerable as the sand which is by the sea shore, were fathered by one man, and him as good as dead."

God instructs us in Ezekiel, "If the wicked person turns from all his sins which he has committed and keeps all My statutes and practices justice and righteousness, he shall certainly live; he shall not die. All his offenses which he has committed will not be remembered against him; because of his righteousness which he has practiced, he will live. Do I take any pleasure in the death of the wicked,' declares the Lord GOD, 'rather than that he would turn from his ways and live?

"But when a righteous person turns away from his righteousness, commits injustice and does according to all the abominations that the wicked person does, will he live? All his righteous deeds which he has done will not be remembered for his treachery which he has committed and his sin which he has committed; for them he will die.

"Therefore I will judge you, house of Israel, each according to his conduct. . . Repent and turn away from all your offenses, so that wrongdoing does not become a stumbling block to you. Hurl away from you all your offenses which you have committed and make yourselves a new heart and a new spirit! For why should you die, house of Israel? For I take no pleasure in the death of anyone who dies. . . Therefore, repent and live!" (Ezekiel 18:21-24, 30-32, NASB).

Walking in the Light

The action of the wicked man that repented, turning away from his wickedness and practicing righteousness merited God's favor. God declares that he shall live. He shall not die.

However, the righteous man that turns away from his righteousness and commits all the abominations of the wicked, does not merit God's favor. He will die for all the sin he has committed. God does not favor the rebellious. However, God does not desire that any would perish. Therefore, repent and live.

God resists the proud, the arrogant, the ones that are so confident that God will never judge them. The Psalmist says, "In all his scheming, the wicked arrogantly thinks: 'There is no accountability'" (Psalm 10:4, HCSB).

However, God gives grace to the humble. Peter advises us, "Likewise, you younger ones, be subject to the elder. Yes, all of you clothe yourselves with humility, to subject yourselves to one another; for 'God resists the proud, but gives grace to the humble.' Humble yourselves therefore under the mighty hand of God, that he may exalt you in due time, casting all your worries on him, because he cares for you.

"Be sober and self-controlled. Be watchful. Your adversary, the devil, walks around like a roaring lion, seeking whom he may devour. Withstand him steadfast in your faith, knowing that your brothers who are in the world are undergoing the same sufferings. But may the God of all grace, who called you to his eternal glory by Christ Jesus, after you have suffered a little while, perfect, establish, strengthen, and settle you" (1 Peter 5:5-10).

Those that walk by faith, those that believe and obey, those that humble themselves merit and receive God's favor. The proud, the arrogant, the sinful, the disobedient, the rebellious, do not merit or receive God's grace, God's favor.

If you are a professing Christian, but have been living by the lusts of the flesh, doing the same things the people in this corrupt sinful world are doing, you need to repent, and you need to repent now. Today is the day of salvation. God tells us in Genesis 6:3, "My Spirit will not strive with man forever."

Tomorrow is promised to no one. Right now, today, may be the last chance you will have to repent of your sinful ways, and turn from them back to God. God is righteous. His ways are just. He rewards the righteous and punishes the wicked.

I don't care what anyone may have told you. If you are walking according to the flesh, you are living in sin. You are unrighteous. The righteous do righteousness (1 John 3:7).

They believe God. They obey God. They do what is right in God's eyes. They deny themselves. They take up their cross and walk in obedience to the leading of the Holy Spirit. They are rewarded with grace in abundance, joy unspeakable, and blessings beyond what our minds can ever imagine.

The unrighteous, the ones that practice unrighteousness, that disobey God, will be held by God for punishment according to how they lived their lives while in this body of flesh. God is no respecter of persons. He will give to each exactly what their deeds have merited.

Chapter 9 Discussion Questions:
No Respecter of Persons

1. What is grace?
2. Who does God give the Holy Spirit to?
3. Upon whom is God's favor poured out?
4. Why did Noah find favor in God's sight?
5. Why did Lot find favor in God's sight?
6. Who does the Lord protect?
7. Who does God hold for punishment on the day of judgment?
8. Why was righteousness credited to Abraham?
9. In whom shall all the families of the earth be blessed?
10. Who did God establish His covenant with?
11. What did God tell Abraham to do with Isaac?
12. How do we know Abraham expected Isaac to return alive with him?

13. How did Abraham reassure Isaac?
14. How did Abraham prove that he feared God?
15. What proves that our belief is genuine?
16. If a wicked person turns from all his sins, why will he live?
17. Why would a righteous man not merit God's favor?
18. Does God give grace to the proud or to the humble?
19. Who merits and receives God's favor?
20. Who are the unrighteous ones?

Chapter 10

Unmerited Favor

"God has imprisoned all in disobedience, so that He may have mercy on all" (Romans 11:32). "He Himself (Christ) is the propitiation for our sins, and not only for ours, but also for those of the whole world" (1 John 2:2). God, by His mercy, has made the forgiveness of sins available to the whole world through Christ's death and resurrection. "For God so loved the world, that He gave His only Son, so that everyone who believes in Him will not perish, but have eternal life." (John 3:16).

While we were still sinners, dead in our sins, Christ died, the righteous for the unrighteous. This was the rich display of God's love and mercy to all who were imprisoned in disobedience. This was God's compassion upon those who had no merit and were only deserving of death. This is God's love and mercy that He extended to the whole world.

However, God only bestows this forgiveness that Christ died for on those who, by exercising their faith to believe in Christ, repent and turn back to Him. By exercising their faith to believe in Jesus, these believers actually receive the forgiveness of sins for which Christ died.

Jesus tells us, "Anyone who believes in Him is not condemned, but anyone who does not believe is already condemned, because he has not believed in the name of the One and Only Son of God" (John 3:18, HCSB). Only those that believe and obey are blessed with actually having their sins forgiven. They are no longer condemned.

Walking in the Light

Those who do not believe are already condemned and will remain condemned unless they believe in the name of Jesus. Their sins will not be forgiven unless they receive God's free gift of mercy by believing and repenting.

Now that we have obeyed the good news, the gospel of the kingdom, we begin to receive of the many blessings that God has prepared for us in Christ. Being reconciled to God, justified by the blood of Christ, having our sins forgiven by His love and mercy, God begins to pour out His grace richly upon those that have obeyed the gospel and joined works of obedience to their faith. It is by this grace that we are now being saved. This grace is God's gift freely given to all who obey Him by exercising their portion of faith to believe in Jesus, the One He sent.

This is the "much more" that Paul speaks of in Romans 5:8-10. "God demonstrates His own love toward us, in that while we were still sinners, Christ died for us. Much more then, having now been justified by His blood, we shall be saved from the wrath of God through Him. For if while we were enemies we were reconciled to God through the death of His Son, much more, having been reconciled, we shall be saved by His life." (NASB).

Paul declares, "For by grace you are being saved through faith which is not your own but instead is a gift from God" (Ephesians 2:8, TFLV). We have been saved by His mercy, having been, by it, reconciled to God through the blood of Christ. We are now in the process of being saved by Christ's life within us. We are now being saved by grace.

This grace is what God is using to save us now in this new and ongoing phase of the salvation process. It is by God's grace that we are being brought on to maturity in Christ and are being purified, sanctified, and enabled to live a godly life in the midst of this corrupt sinful world. We are, right now, in this life, enabled by the leading and empowering of the Holy Spirit to live as Jesus lived, to walk as Jesus walked, fully pleasing to the Father.

This, now, is where we need to exercise the portion of faith that God has given to each of us. We believed God for our initial salvation of being restored to fellowship with God by the blood of Jesus. We now need to exercise our faith to continue to believe God. We must believe that the life of Christ indwelling us as the Holy Spirit in our spirit, is able to, not only liberate us from the bondage to sin, but to lead us to walk in continual obedience, abiding in Christ, doing the will of the Father, and not fulfilling the lust of the flesh.

This indwelling Holy Spirit will teach us all that is ours in Christ. He will cause us to know the hope of glory that is ours. "Christ in you, the hope of glory" (Colossians 1:27). As we look to Jesus, He will cause us to know the power of His resurrection and the fellowship of His sufferings that we might attain unto the first, or best, resurrection (Revelation 20:5-6).

This is God's grace, the gift of His Holy Spirit given to live within every born-again believer. This power of God, working mightily within us to accomplish His will, produces within us a deep lasting sense of love, joy, and peace.

Once anyone responds to God's compassion, His free offer of love and mercy, by obeying God and believing in the one He sent, God immediately pours out His grace upon them. He cleanses them from their sins. He sets them free from the condemnation of slavery to sin and fills the cleansed vessel with His Holy Spirit. This power of God works in the believer's life filling them with unexplainable joy, restoring them to fellowship with God by empowering them to hear God and obey God,.

They are baptized by the Holy Spirit into Christ and thereby baptized into the death of Christ. They are buried together with Him by baptism into His death.

"What shall we say then? Shall we continue in sin, that grace may abound? May it never be! We who died to sin, how could we live in it any longer? Or don't you know that all we who were baptized into Christ Jesus were baptized into his death? We were buried therefore with him through baptism into death, that just as Christ was raised from the dead through

Walking in the Light

the glory of the Father, so we also might walk in newness of life.

"For if we have become united with him in the likeness of his death, we will also be part of his resurrection; knowing this, that our old man was crucified with him, that the body of sin might be done away with, so that we would no longer be in bondage to sin. . . . Thus consider yourselves also to be dead to sin, but alive to God in Christ Jesus our Lord" (Romans 6: 1-6, 11).

God shows His favor, His grace, to the righteous, to those that love Him, to those that obey Him, to those that humble themselves before Him. God's favor is demonstrated to them by Him giving them His power, the power of the resurrection, in the person of Christ, as the Holy Spirit, to dwell with in their spirit.

This indwelling Spirit, the Spirit of Christ, enters into the believer's spirit and makes it alive, filling the believer with an indescribable deep, lasting inner joy. This blessing bestowed by God on those who, by believing, have found favor in His sight, and the resulting joy produced in the believer's heart is referred to in the scriptures as grace.

It is this grace that works in the believer's heart to produce the experience referred to in Romans 5 as the "much more" than being reconciled to God. This "much more" is the process that we begin to experience after we are saved, after we are born again. This is the life of Christ working mightily within us through the indwelling Holy Spirit to transform us and conform us to the image of Christ (Ephesians 3:16-21).

This is the beginning of the process referred to in scripture as the salvation of our soul. "You love Him (Jesus), though you have not seen Him. And though not seeing Him now, you believe in Him and rejoice with inexpressible and glorious joy, because you are receiving the goal of your faith, the salvation of your souls" (1 Peter 1:8-9). This is the goal of our faith!

When the entire context of scripture is considered with an open and honest heart, humbling ourselves by laying aside all preconceptions and the doctrines of man, it becomes obvious that the one thing that is never meant by the word 'grace' is 'unmerited favor.'

Let's try demonstrating this by substituting unmerited favor for grace in a few verses. Genesis 6:8-9 says, "But Noah found grace in the eyes of the LORD . . . Noah was a righteous man, blameless in his generation. Noah walked with God." This passage could be rephrased as "But Noah found unmerited favor in the eyes of the LORD . . . Noah was a righteous man, blameless in his generation. Noah walked with God." This does not make sense. Unmerited does not fit with righteous, blameless, and walking with God.

Luke 2:40 says, "The child (Jesus) was growing, and was becoming strong in spirit, being filled with wisdom, and the grace of God was upon him." This verse could be rephrased as "The child (Jesus) was growing, and was becoming strong in spirit, being filled with wisdom, and the unmerited favor of God was upon him." It is hard to believe that Jesus, The Son in whom God was well pleased did not merit God's favor. Truly, God's favor bestowed on Jesus was merited. God was well pleased with His Son.

Galatians 5:4 says, "You are alienated from Christ, you who desire to be justified by the law. You have fallen away from grace." This verse could be rephrased as, "You are alienated from Christ, you who desire to be justified by the law. You have fallen away from unmerited favor."

If God's favor is unmerited, how is it possible to fall from it? You fall from God's favor when you do something that is displeasing to Him.

Grace is never unmerited favor. God's unmerited compassion toward a sinful world is His mercy sent to us in the person of Jesus Christ. Grace is God's merited favor made freely available to those who, by exercising their faith, believe in Jesus.

The teaching that grace is unmerited favor leads professing Christians to believe that it does not matter how they live. It turns the grace of God into promiscuity, and a license for immorality. This is exactly what is happening in many churches today.

Jude testified to this very fact. "For some men, who were designated for this judgment long ago, have come in by stealth; they are ungodly, turning the grace of our God into promiscuity and denying Jesus Christ, our only Master and Lord" (Jude 4, HCSB).

Some that have embraced the idea that grace is unmerited favor believe that they received eternal life at the time they first believed. However, scripture records Jesus saying, "Most certainly I tell you, there is no one who has left house, or wife, or brothers, or parents, or children, for God's Kingdom's sake, who will not receive many times more in this time, and in the world to come, eternal life" (Luke 18:29-30). If they remain faithful, they will receive eternal life in the next age, the world to come.

Paul writes, "Laying up in store for themselves a good foundation against the time to come, that they may lay hold on eternal life" (1 Timothy 6:19). Why would we need to lay hold of something that we have already received?

Paul continues, "He poured out this Spirit on us abundantly through Jesus Christ our Savior, so that having been justified by His grace, we may become heirs with the hope of eternal life" (Titus 3:6-7). Why would we be hoping for something that we already have received?

Again Paul explains, "Just as sin reigned in death, so also grace will reign through righteousness, resulting in eternal life through Jesus Christ our Lord" (Romans 5:21). How can grace reigning through righteousness result in eternal life if we have already received that eternal life?

Many also believe that all their sins, past, present, and future are forgiven at the moment they believe. Therefore, they believe that they, as those that are in Christ, will never experience condemnation. God will never convict them for any sin that might be in their lives. Therefore, they believe they will never experience guilt for sin.

The apostle John exposes these lies, "If we say that we have no sin, we are deceiving ourselves and the truth is not in us. If we confess our sins, He is faithful and righteous, so that He will forgive us our sins and cleanse us from all unrighteousness. If we say that we have not sinned, we make Him a liar and His word is not in us" (1 John 1:8-10). If all our sins, past, present, and future have been forgiven, why does John, writing to believers, tell us that we need to confess our sins so that He will forgive us our sins?

Unfortunately for these people, the scriptures do not say all our sins, past, present and future are forgiven when we first believe. In fact, we are told that it is our sins committed previous to believing that are forgiven. "The person who lacks these things is blind and shortsighted, and has forgotten the cleansing from his past sins" (2 Peter 1:9, HCSB).

If they ever experience any guilt or condemnation for sin, they might say, "It must be from the enemy, the accuser of the brethren," and therefore reject it as an attack from Satan. Some even claim that they never need to repent for any sin after being saved. If, in fact, all their sins, past, present, and future have been taken away and forgiven by the blood of Christ that was shed for them, it would be a demonstration of unbelief to repent of any sins ever again.

However, in chapters two and three of the book of Revelation, Jesus sends letters to seven churches. In five of the letters to these believers, He commands them to repent. If all of their sins, past, present, and future have already been forgiven and they never again need to repent, why would Jesus command them to repent?

Many people that believe that grace is God's unmerited favor are not overly troubled by sin in their lives. In fact, they justify their sinful lifestyles by the teaching that Paul's account in Romans 7:13-24 is his testimony of his life as a born-again Christian. Paul states in this account that he is unspiritual, a slave to sin, that he has no ability to do the good that he desires to do, and that he practices the evil that he does not want to do.

Walking in the Light

Therefore, those that follow this teaching of grace will say, "See I am not so bad. Paul's Christian life was a continual struggle with sin. I myself sin all the time. I am continually sinning. This is the expected life for a Christian living in this sinful world."

As we have seen in a previous chapter, Paul was writing in Romans chapter seven about the merely natural man, the unspiritual man, who had agreed with the law of God that it was good and set out to do that good. He found that he was enslaved to sin. He found that he had no ability to do the good that he desired to do. Ultimately, he realized that rather than doing the good that he wanted to do, he ended up practicing the evil that he did not want to do.

Those that profess to be Christians, but have never been born again, being unspiritual, merely natural men, find themselves in exactly this same predicament that Paul describes in Romans chapter seven. It is not until they realize the hopelessness of their situation and cry out in desperation to God for deliverance that they can be liberated by the power of God in the Spirit of Christ coming into their spirit and making it alive.

Because they do not understand the scriptures or the power of God, those that believe grace is unmerited favor are badly deceived. They have totally missed the fundamental essence of the good news, the gospel of Jesus Christ. They do not realize that Jesus died to destroy the power of the devil. Jesus died and was raised up by the power of God to set us free from bondage to sin and empower us to live holy lives in all humility and obedience now, in the midst of this sinful world.

By baptism into Christ's death through the Holy Spirit, we died with Christ and have been released from bondage to sin. Sin no longer has dominion over us. By the power of the resurrection, we have been raised up with Christ to walk in newness of life. It is the gift of God, the indwelling Holy Spirit, the Spirit of the glorified Christ that now empowers us to live holy lives, lives pleasing to God in all obedience.

God is no fool. He gives His grace to those that are pleasing in His sight. He gives His grace to those that believe Him, to those that by faith obey Him. He rewards the righteous, the faithful that endure to the end. We are told in Acts 5:32, "We are witnesses of these things; and so is the Holy Spirit, whom God has given to those who obey Him."

What greater favor can God bestow on believers than to give them His Holy Spirit? Notice, however, that God gives His Holy Spirit to those that have merited it by obeying Him. What an incredible blessing for simply obeying Him by repenting and turning from darkness to light, from Satan to God!

He punishes the unrighteous, the disobedient, the rebellious, those that practice sin. God is righteous and His ways are just. "God is no respecter of persons" (Acts 10:34, KJV). He rewards each person with what their lives merit, with what they deserve based on what they have done in the body, whether good or bad.

Paul writes to the believers in Corinth warning them to be careful about how they live. "For we must all appear before the judgment seat of Christ, so that each of us may receive what is due us for the things done while in the body, whether good or bad" (2 Corinthians 5:10, NIV).

A person's belief in God is demonstrated by his obedience to God. John reveals this truth, "We know that we have come to know him if we keep his commands. Whoever says, 'I know him,' but does not do what he commands is a liar, and the truth is not in that person. But if anyone obeys his word, love for God is truly made complete in them. This is how we know we are in him: Whoever claims to live in him must live as Jesus did" (1 John 2:3-6).

Mercy is God's unmerited compassion offered freely to the whole world. Grace is God's favor to those that merit it; to those that believe Him, to those that obey Him, to those with whom He is pleased.

Words have meaning. To understand scripture, we must understand the meaning of the words used in scripture

Walking in the Light

according to what the author, directed by the Holy Spirit, intended them to mean. We must not assign some other meaning to words to support some doctrine of men that we may have been taught and embraced.

We must turn away from any teaching that the scriptures have demonstrated to be false. If we repent, change our mind about and turn away from these false teachings, and return to the truth of scripture, purifying ourselves, we will become useful vessels for our Master. Paul assures us, "So if anyone purifies himself from these things (false teachings), he will be a special instrument, set apart, useful to the Master, prepared for every good work (2 Timothy 2:21, HCSB).

God expects His people to live holy lives. He expects this because He has given us His Holy Spirit to enable us to do this. Peter reveals this glorious truth saying, "His divine power has given us everything required for life and godliness through the knowledge of Him who called us by His own glory and goodness. By these He has given us very great and precious promises, so that through them you may share in the divine nature, escaping the corruption that is in the world because of evil desires" (2 Peter 1:3-4, HCSB).

It is not by our power, but it is by the power of God within us. When we walk by the Spirit, we are empowered to live holy lives. "Walk by the Spirit, and you won't fulfill the lust of the flesh" (Galatians 5:16).

We must continue to believe God. We must continue to believe that He is able to do everything He has promised. We must believe that the power He is causing to work mightily within us as believers is fully able to empower us to live holy lives in full obedience to Him.

All God is asking from us is to live by faith, remaining in Christ, trusting in His mighty power to work according to His great strength to transform us and conform us to His image, doing His will through us as we endure to the end, fixing our eyes on Jesus. As we do this, His grace will fill us with a deep, abiding joy, and that joy will be our strength. It will enable us to remain steadfast to the end!

Are you walking by faith? Are you believing God is able to empower you to live a holy life in the midst of this crooked and perverse world? Are you finding God's grace to be sufficient for your every need, or are you still struggling with sin in your life?

Have you experienced the liberation from the power of sin that God's grace provides, or are you still a slave to sin? If you are still in bondage to sin, perhaps you should test yourself to see if you are truly in the faith.

Paul commands professing Christians to test themselves to see if they are truly in the faith. "Examine yourselves to see whether you are in the faith; test yourselves. Do you not realize that Christ Jesus is in you—unless, of course, you fail the test?" (2 Corinthians 13:5, NIV). "If anyone does not have the Spirit of Christ, he does not belong to Him" (Romans 8:9, NASB).

Chapter 10 Discussion Questions:
Unmerited Favor

1. Why did God imprison everyone in disobedience?
2. Whose sins did Christ die for?
3. When did Christ die for our sins?
4. Whose sins did the righteous One die for?
5. Who receives forgiveness of their sins?
6. Upon whom does God pour out His grace?
7. What is the "much more" than being reconciled to God that Paul spoke of in Romans 5?
8. Having been saved by His mercy, His unmerited compassion, what are we now being saved by?
9. Having been saved, what do we now need to exercise our faith to believe?
10. What will teach us all that is ours in Christ?
11. When we are baptized by the Spirit into Christ, what are we baptized into?

Walking in the Light

12. Who does God show His favor, His grace, to?
13. What is the one thing that the scriptures never mean by the word 'grace'?
14. If grace is unmerited favor, how can you fall from it?
15. What turns the grace of God into promiscuity?
16. According to Luke 18:29-30, when is eternal life received?
17. If believer's sins, past, present, and future have all been forgiven, why does Jesus tell the believers in five of the seven letters to the churches to repent?
18. What did the unspiritual, merely natural man in Romans seven learn when he set out to do the good that he agreed with in the law of God?
19. Who does God give grace to?
20. What word is used in scripture to refer to God's unmerited compassion?
21. What word is used in scripture to refer to God's merited favor?
22. Why does God expect His people to live holy lives?
23. As believers, what is God asking us to believe now?
24. What is the test of whether we are in the faith, of whether we belong to Christ?

Chapter 11

Eternal Security

The concept of eternal security is often referred to as 'once saved, always saved.' The basic idea of this teaching is that once you are saved, once you become a Christian, then you are always saved. You, therefore, cannot lose your salvation. Your future in heaven is eternally secure. This teaching is very popular in many churches today.

Some that hold to this teaching believe that faith in Christ is intellectual assent. Their idea of faith requires no commitment, no decision of the will, no turning from sins, and no works that are part of faith in Christ. They claim that if you are convinced or persuaded that what He promised is true, then you believe in Him. They teach that turning from sins, commitment, obedience, and perseverance are not faith and thus are not conditions of eternal life.

However, according to scripture, there is much more to saving faith than intellectual assent to a historical fact. Saving faith in Christ produces dramatic change in the character and the life of the believer. It produces repentance, a turning away from darkness, sin, Satan, and self, and a turning back to God demonstrated by a life of obedience, being empowered by the indwelling Holy Spirit.

The Gospel of John tells us, "There was a man from the Pharisees named Nicodemus, a ruler of the Jews. This man came to Him (Jesus) at night and said, 'Rabbi, we know that You have come from God as a teacher, for no one could perform these signs You do unless God were with him.'

"Jesus replied, 'I assure you: Unless someone is born again, he cannot see the kingdom of God.'

"'But how can anyone be born when he is old?' Nicodemus asked Him. 'Can he enter his mother's womb a second time and be born?'

"Jesus answered, 'I assure you: Unless someone is born of water and the Spirit, he cannot enter the kingdom of God. Whatever is born of the flesh is flesh, and whatever is born of the Spirit is spirit'" (John 3:1-6, HCSB).

Jesus makes this simple truth so clear that anyone could understand it. Unless we are born again we cannot even see the kingdom of God. It is not enough to be born of the flesh and to have studied all of scripture from Genesis to Revelation. Unless we are born again we cannot even perceive or understand the kingdom of God.

It is enough to be born of water, born of the flesh, one time. We do not need to enter our mother's womb a second time and be born of the flesh again. This second birth that Jesus speaks of is not to be born of the flesh again.

The second birth that Jesus speaks of is referring to the need to be born of the Spirit. Our spirit must be born of the Holy Spirit. The Holy Spirit must enter into our spirit and make it alive. When He does, we become a new creation.

Paul confirms this saying, "Therefore, if anyone is in Christ, he is a new creation; old things have passed away, and look, new things have come" (2 Corinthians 5:17, HCSB). When we are born again, we receive a new power, a new source of life that we can live by. Before we were born again, we had one controlling power within us that we could live by, that was our flesh, and that flesh was in bondage to the sin that dwelt within it.

Before we were born again, our experience was exactly like that described by Paul in Romans chapter seven. "I am made out of flesh, sold into sin's power. . . The desire to do what is good is with me, but there is no ability to do it. . . But I practice the evil that I do not want to do" (Romans 7:14, 18-19).

When we are born again, a new powerful life, in the person of the Holy Spirit, enters into us, into our spirit. This powerful life-giving Spirit makes our spirit alive. Its power is greater than that of the sin that dwells in our flesh.

This Spirit's powerful law of life in Christ Jesus breaks the power of sin to control us. It sets us free from the law of sin and of death. It sets us free from bondage to sin. Sin no longer has dominion over us. We are no longer under the condemnation of slavery to sin.

Paul explains this in Romans 8:1-2. "There is therefore now no condemnation to those who are in Christ Jesus, who don't walk according to the flesh, but according to the Spirit. For the law of the Spirit of life in Christ Jesus made me free from the law of sin and of death."

This power of the law of life in Christ Jesus is stronger than the power of the law of sin and of death in our flesh. It has broken sin's hold over us and has set us free to walk in a new way of life.

Paul describes this liberation from the power of sin in detail in Romans 6:3-7,11. "Or don't you know that all we who were baptized into Christ Jesus were baptized into his death? We were buried therefore with him through baptism into death, that just as Christ was raised from the dead through the glory of the Father, so we also might walk in newness of life.

"For if we have become united with him in the likeness of his death, we will also be part of his resurrection; knowing this, that our old man was crucified with him, that the body of sin might be done away with, so that we would no longer be in bondage to sin. For he who has died has been freed from sin... Thus consider yourselves also to be dead to sin, but alive to God in Christ Jesus our Lord."

Paul continues this thought saying, "Don't you know that when you offer yourselves to someone as obedient slaves, you are slaves of the one you obey—whether you are slaves to sin, which leads to death, or to obedience, which leads to righteousness? But thanks be to God that, though you used to be slaves to sin, you have come to obey from your heart the pattern of teaching that has now claimed your allegiance.

"You have been set free from sin and have become slaves to righteousness. . . But now that you have been set free from sin and have become slaves of God, the benefit you reap leads to holiness, and the result is eternal life" (Romans 6:17-18, 22).

We now become active participants in a spiritual battle. Both sin in our flesh and the Spirit's law of life in Christ Jesus working in our spirit are striving to gain superiority in the life of the born-again believer. The outcome of this battle is determined by the choices we make, every moment, every day.

Paul describes this battle in his letter to the churches in Galatia. "For the flesh desires what is contrary to the Spirit, and the Spirit what is contrary to the flesh. They are in conflict with each other, so that you are not to do whatever you want" (Galatians 5:17, NIV).

Paul warns us in verses 19-21 about the seriousness of how we live. "Now the deeds of the flesh are obvious, which are: adultery, sexual immorality, uncleanness, lustfulness, idolatry, sorcery, hatred, strife, jealousies, outbursts of anger, rivalries, divisions, heresies, envy, murders, drunkenness, orgies, and things like these; of which I forewarn you, even as I also forewarned you, that those who practice such things will not inherit God's Kingdom."

The deeds of the flesh are sin. If we practice sinning, if we continually sin we will not inherit God's kingdom.

However, if we walk by the Spirit, our living will be holy and we will be pleasing to God. Paul encourages us in Galatians 5:16, "But I say, walk by the Spirit, and you won't fulfill the lust of the flesh."

Paul reminds us, "For those who live according to the flesh set their minds on the things of the flesh, but those who live according to the Spirit, the things of the Spirit. For the mind of the flesh is death, but the mind of the Spirit is life and peace; because the mind of the flesh is hostile toward God; for it is not subject to God's law, neither indeed can it be. Those who are in the flesh can't please God" (Romans 8:6-8).

Paul makes an astounding declaration in verse nine, "But you are not in the flesh but in the Spirit, if it is so that the Spirit of God dwells in you. But if any man doesn't have the Spirit of Christ, he is not his." (Romans 8:9). If you do not have the Spirit of Christ, you do not belong to Him. You are not a genuine Christian unless you are born again, born from above, born of the Spirit.

Do not be deceived. You are not in the Spirit unless the Spirit of Christ is in you. If the Holy Spirit does not live in you, you are not truly a Christian, you are still in the flesh. It does not matter what you believe, if the Spirit of Christ is not in you, you are none of His. You must be born again, born from above, born of the Spirit.

The apostle John instructs us as to how we can know if we are genuine Christians. "By this we know that we have come to know Him, if we keep His commandments. The one who says, 'I have come to know Him,' and does not keep His commandments, is a liar, and the truth is not in him; but whoever follows His word, in him the love of God has truly been perfected. By this we know that we are in Him: the one who says that he remains in Him ought, himself also, walk just as He (Jesus) walked" (1 John 2:1-6, NASB).

The apostle John continues to warn us, "Everyone who practices sin also practices lawlessness; and sin is lawlessness. You know that He appeared in order to take away sins; and in Him there is no sin. No one who remains in Him sins continually; no one who sins continually has seen Him or knows Him. Little children, make sure no one deceives you; the one who practices righteousness is righteous, just as He is righteous; the one who practices sin is of the devil; for the devil has been sinning from the beginning.

"The Son of God appeared for this purpose, to destroy the works of the devil. No one who has been born of God practices sin, because His seed remains in him; and he cannot sin continually, because he has been born of God. By this

Walking in the Light

the children of God and the children of the devil are obvious: anyone who does not practice righteousness is not of God, nor the one who does not love his brother and sister" (1 John 3:4-10, NASB).

If someone's professed salvation experience contradicts the entire counsel of scripture, they are not really saved. If we have been deceived into thinking we are saved, when the scriptures assure us that we are not, then the teaching of 'once saved, always saved' is irrelevant. The teaching of eternal security for that person would more accurately be expressed as 'never saved, still lost.'

The gospel presented in scripture always requires a decision on the part of the hearer, to believe or not to believe. If they are persuaded that Jesus has been made both Lord and Christ, that He died sacrificially, in our place, and that by the power of the resurrection, He was raised up from the dead, never to die again, they can by faith, repent and be baptized by the Holy Spirit into Christ. By that baptism, they receive the Holy Spirit into their spirit and thereby become a new creation, liberated, set free from slavery to sin to walk in newness of life. By this baptism they are empowered by the Spirit, enabled to walk in joyful obedience to God.

The reality of this salvation experience is demonstrated in the life of the believer by doing works worthy of repentance, by loving one another and by bearing fruit of the Spirit. You will know the tree by the fruit it bears. They will no longer glory in sin, but they will be ashamed of that in which they formerly lived. They will no longer maintain a form of religion, while denying the power of God that is able to set them free from slavery to sin.

Rather, they will glory in the power of God working within them to sanctify them, making them holy in all their conduct as the one who calls them is holy. They will experience unspeakable joy as they yield themselves fully to Christ Jesus their Lord, and allow Him, by His indwelling Holy Spirit, to transform them by the renewing of their minds, placing His desires into their hearts, conforming them to His image.

Now, for someone who has had such a genuine salvation experience of being born again, being born of the Spirit, and having escaped the corruption of the world through the knowledge of our Lord and Savior Jesus Christ, we can consider the validity of the teaching, once saved, always saved.

Chapter 11 Discussion Questions:
Eternal Security

1. By what name is the concept of eternal security often referred to?
2. What is the basic idea of "once saved, always saved"?
3. What does saving faith produce in the life of a believer?
4. What did Jesus tell Nicodemas?
5. What does it mean to be born again, born of the Spirit, or born from above?
6. What controlled how we lived before we were born again? What did it cause us to do?
7. How is a person able to be set free from the condemnation of slavery to sin?
8. What breaks the power of sin's control over us when we are born again?
9. Why should a born again believer consider themselves dead to sin?
10. Why was our old man crucified with Christ?
11. When do we become participants in a spiritual battle?
12. What decides the outcome of this spiritual battle?
13. What two forces are fighting to gain superiority in the life of a believer?
14. What is the destiny of those who practice the deeds of the flesh?
15. What prevents us from fulfilling the lusts of the flesh?
16. What is required for someone to be a genuine Christian?

Walking in the Light

17. What does 1 John say about someone that does not practice righteousness, but practices sin?
18. What does the gospel found in scripture always require?
19. How Is the reality of the salvation experience demonstrated in the life of a believer?

Chapter 12

No One Can Take Us Out of His Hand

To begin our consideration of this teaching of once saved, always saved, as with any other teaching, we must begin with all humility, being willing to lay aside all preconceptions based on what men have taught us. We must have such a deep desire to know the truth, that we are willing to let the Holy Spirit and the scriptures be the final authority to arbitrate between truth and error.

Now, let us prayerfully allow the Holy Spirit to direct us and to teach us. We will begin by considering some of the passages that are used to support the "once saved, always saved" teaching. Let's start by examining the passage in John 10:27-30.

"My sheep hear my voice, and I know them, and they follow me. I give eternal life to them. They will never perish, and no one will snatch them out of my hand. My Father who has given them to me is greater than all. No one is able to snatch them out of my Father's hand. I and the Father are one."

To understand this passage, it is important to pay close attention to the sequence of events that Jesus mentions. First, His sheep hear His voice. This attentiveness by the sheep to His voice enables Jesus to develop a relationship with them. He describes this relationship with His sheep saying, "I know them."

As a result of this relationship, His sheep follow Him. Because of the intimacy of His relationship with His sheep, His sheep obediently follow Him. They follow Him because

Walking in the Light

their love for Him produces a desire to please Him in all things. The result of their faithfully following Him is that He gives them eternal life.

We now need to focus on the time when each of these events takes place. Turning to Mark 10:29-30 will help us with this. "Jesus said, 'Most certainly I tell you, there is no one who has left house, or brothers, or sisters, or father, or mother, or wife, or children, or land, for my sake, and for the sake of the Good News, but he will receive one hundred times more now in this time: houses, brothers, sisters, mothers, children, and land, with persecutions; and in the age to come eternal life.'"

We see this again in Luke 18:29. Jesus said to His disciples, "Most certainly I tell you, there is no one who has left house, or wife, or brothers, or parents, or children, for God's Kingdom's sake, who will not receive many times more in this time, and in the world to come, eternal life."

In each of these passages, the events are laid out in the same sequence. These people hear the Lord's voice and enter into a relationship with Him that results in them following Him, even to the point of leaving spouse, parents, children, or siblings. They trust Him so much that they gladly follow Him, leaving houses and lands for His sake, even while enduring persecutions in this life. Then in the next age, in the world to come, they receive eternal life.

In light of this time frame for these events, we can take a fresh look at this passage in John 10. In the world to come, in the new Jerusalem, on the new earth the faithful believers will receive the promised inheritance of eternal life.

In Genesis 3:22-24 we read, "And the LORD God said, 'The man has now become like one of us, knowing good and evil. He must not be allowed to reach out his hand and take also from the tree of life and eat, and live forever.' So the LORD God banished him (man) from the Garden of Eden to work the ground from which he had been taken. After he drove the man out, he placed on the east side of the Garden of Eden cherubim and a flaming sword flashing back and forth to guard the way to the tree of life."

According to this passage, it is by eating the fruit of the tree of life that man can receive eternal life and live forever. The righteous God could not allow the sinful man to eat from the tree of life and live forever. Therefore God drove man from the Garden of Eden and blocked the way to the tree of live by placing cherubim there with a flaming sword.

In His letter to the church in Ephesus, Jesus says, "The one who has an ear, let him hear what the Spirit says to the churches. To the one who overcomes, I will grant to eat from the tree of life, which is in the Paradise of God" (Revelation 2:7, NASB).

John writes in Revelation 22:1-2, "He showed me a river of water of life, clear as crystal, proceeding out of the throne of God and of the Lamb, in the middle of its street. On this side of the river and on that was the tree of life, bearing twelve kinds of fruits, yielding its fruit every month. The leaves of the tree were for the healing of the nations."

Finally, in Revelation 22:14-15 we read, "Blessed are those who do his commandments, that they may have the right to the tree of life, and may enter in by the gates into the city. Outside are the dogs, the sorcerers, the sexually immoral, the murderers, the idolaters, and everyone who loves and practices falsehood."

We see from these passages that the tree of life that was available to man in the Garden of Eden before he sinned and rebelled against God is now again made available to any person who by faith in Christ continues to walk in obedience to the leading of the indwelling Holy Spirit. The one that overcomes, enduring to the end, remaining steadfast, holding firm to the confidence that he had received in the beginning, will be granted access to the tree of life in the new Jerusalem and receive eternal life.

Only the overcoming believer, the one who washed his robes by persevering in faith, abiding in Christ, are allowed the right to the tree of life and to enter the city, the new Jerusalem. Outside are those that continued practicing sin. They have forfeited their right to the tree of life and the right

Walking in the Light

to enter the holy city. They did not live their lives in this age in a manner worthy of the kingdom.

Now we can understand why those that Jesus has given eternal life to can never be taken out of His hand. No one can take them out of His hand or the Father's hand because the faithful, victorious believers are now safely inside the heavenly kingdom. Their destiny is finally secure. They are no longer in the body of flesh wherein sin dwells. They are no longer tempted by Satan. His power has been destroyed, he has been cast into the lake of fire,.

Now we can see that this passage in John 10 is not referring to believers in this age being eternally secure. Our eternal destiny is secure when we have gained entrance into the heavenly kingdom and have obtained the right to take of the tree of life in the new Jerusalem.

Paul explains his understanding of this in Philippians 3:12-15. "Not that I have already obtained, or am already made perfect; but I press on, that I may take hold of that for which also I was taken hold of by Christ Jesus.

"Brothers, I don't regard myself as yet having taken hold, but one thing I do: forgetting the things which are behind, and stretching forward to the things which are before, I press on toward the goal for the prize of the high calling of God in Christ Jesus. Let us therefore, as many as are perfect, think this way."

Again Paul expresses his awareness that his eternal destiny has not been secured. "Everyone who competes in the games goes into strict training. They do it to get a crown that will not last, but we do it to get a crown that will last forever. Therefore I do not run like someone running aimlessly; I do not fight like a boxer beating the air. No, I strike a blow to my body and make it my slave so that after I have preached to others, I myself will not be disqualified for the prize" (1 Corinthians 9:25-27, NIV).

Paul was keenly aware that even though he relentlessly preached the gospel to others, his eternal destiny was not secure. He fully understood the definite possibility of being disqualified from winning the prize that he so desperately sought, if he did not endure to the end, faithfully abiding in Christ.

Paul writes to the believers in the church in Colossae explaining to them that they have been qualified to share in the inheritance of God's holy people in the kingdom of light. His prayer is that they would be filled with a knowledge of God's will that they might live lives worthy of the Lord, being pleasing to Him in all things. He is concerned that they would not be ignorant of God's will and that they would not live carelessly and become disqualified from that wonderful inheritance.

"We continually ask God to fill you with the knowledge of his will through all the wisdom and understanding that the Spirit gives, so that you may live a life worthy of the Lord and please him in every way: bearing fruit in every good work, growing in the knowledge of God, being strengthened with all power according to his glorious might so that you may have great endurance and patience, and giving joyful thanks to the Father, who has qualified you to share in the inheritance of his holy people in the kingdom of light" (Colossians 1:9-12).

In Matthew 24 Jesus tells us that the good news of the gospel is simply this, "He that endures to the end shall be saved." At the beginning of this chapter the disciples were pointing out to Jesus the majesty of the temple buildings and Jesus replied to them that not a stone of the buildings would be left that would not be thrown down.

So the disciples approached Jesus privately, while He was sitting on the Mount of Olives, and asked Him to explain to them three things. "Tell us, when will these things be? What is the sign of your coming, and of the end of the age?"

At the end of the first part of His answer to them Jesus says, "This Good News of the Kingdom will be preached in the whole world for a testimony to all the nations, and then the end will come." Now, as you read through Jesus' reply to them, pay close attention and tell me as soon as you hear something that is "Good News." Okay, here we go!

Walking in the Light

Jesus answered them, "Be careful that no one leads you astray. For many will come in my name, saying, 'I am the Christ,' and will lead many astray. You will hear of wars and rumors of wars. See that you aren't troubled, for all this must happen, but the end is not yet. For nation will rise against nation, and kingdom against kingdom; and there will be famines, plagues, and earthquakes in various places. But all these things are the beginning of birth pains.

"Then they will deliver you up to oppression and will kill you. You will be hated by all of the nations for my name's sake. Then many will stumble, and will deliver up one another, and will hate one another. Many false prophets will arise and will lead many astray. Because iniquity will be multiplied, the love of many will grow cold. But he who endures to the end will be saved. This Good News of the Kingdom will be preached in the whole world for a testimony to all the nations, and then the end will come" (Matthew 24:4-14).

That's right! That is the good news Jesus referred to. "He who endures to the end will be saved." This good news of the Kingdom will be proclaimed throughout the entire world as a testimony to every nation, then the end will come. We need to proclaim this good news. Believers must understand the necessity of faithfully enduring to the end.

Paul tells the believers in the church in Thessalonica that he boasts in the other churches about them. He writes, "We ourselves glory in you in the churches of God for your patience and faith in all your persecutions and tribulations that ye endure: Which is a manifest token of the righteous judgment of God, that ye may be counted worthy of the kingdom of God, for which ye also suffer: (2 Thessalonians 1:4-5, KJV).

Paul speaks in 1 Corinthians 9:24 about a race that we are in. He says, "Don't you know that those who run in a race all run, but one receives the prize? Run like that, that you may win."

Again, in Hebrews 12:1-2, we are told that we are in a race. "Therefore let's also, seeing we are surrounded by so great a cloud of witnesses, lay aside every weight and the sin which so easily entangles us, and let's run with perseverance the race that is set before us, looking to Jesus, the author and perfecter of faith, who for the joy that was set before him endured the cross, despising its shame, and has sat down at the right hand of the throne of God."

We start this race by being born again. That is how everyone starts. This race continues from the time we are born of the Spirit until we go to meet the Lord, whether through death or at His coming.

Once we are born again, the most crucial thing we must keep in mind is the absolute necessity of enduring to the end, that we finish the race, that we finish our course. We must lay aside every weight and the sin which so easily entangles us and run with perseverance.

We do this by looking away to Jesus, by keeping our focus on Him. We do this by encouraging one another daily, while it is called today, so that none of us is hardened by sin's deception, so that none of us fall into the same pattern of disobedience as those that rebelled and fell in the desert.

The writer of Hebrews warns us, "Beware, brothers, lest perhaps there might be in any one of you an evil heart of unbelief, in falling away from the living God; but exhort one another day by day, so long as it is called 'today', lest any one of you be hardened by the deceitfulness of sin. For we have become partakers of Christ, if we hold the beginning of our confidence firm to the end" (Hebrews 3:12-14).

Paul again writes to the church in Thessalonica, "This is an obvious sign of the righteous judgment of God, to the end that you may be counted worthy of God's Kingdom, for which you also suffer. Since it is a righteous thing with God to repay affliction to those who afflict you, and to give relief to you who are afflicted with us, when the Lord Jesus is revealed from heaven with his mighty angels in flaming fire, punishing those who don't know God, and to those who don't obey the Good News of our Lord Jesus, who will pay the penalty: eternal destruction from the face of the Lord and from the glory of his might, when he comes in that day to be glorified in his saints and to be admired among all those who have believed, because our testimony to you was believed" (2 Thessalonians 1:5-10).

Paul finishes his course saying, "For I am already being offered, and the time of my departure has come. I have fought the good fight. I have finished the course. I have kept the faith. From now on, the crown of righteousness is stored up for me, which the Lord, the righteous judge, will give to me on that day; and not to me only, but also to all those who have loved his appearing" (2 Timothy 4:6-8).

It is only after we have completed our life in this body, after we have run our race and stood before the judgment seat of Christ on the day of the Lord, and been found worthy of the kingdom that we will be granted the right to enter into that city, the new Jerusalem. It is then that we will have access to the tree of life. It is then that we shall inherit all the promises made to the faithful overcoming believers. It is then that we will be able to eat of the fruit of the tree of life that we might finally receive that eternal life that we have long hoped for.

Our eternal destiny is very much dependent on our continuing to abide in Christ, enduring faithfully to the end. This is the good news of the kingdom that needs to be preached throughout the entire world, then the end shall come.

Chapter 12 Discussion Questions:
No One Can Take Us Out of His Hand

1. Why do His sheep follow Jesus?
2. What is the result of the sheep faithfully following Jesus?
3. What did Jesus promise to those that leave families and property for the kingdom's sake?
4. What could these followers expect to receive in this age, and what in the next?
5. Why did God block the way to the tree of life in Genesis 3?

6. In Revelation 2, what did Jesus promise to the overcomers in the church in Ephesus?
7. Where is the tree of life in Revelation 22?
8. Who does Revelation 22 say will have right to the tree of life?
9. Who is allowed to enter in by the gates into the city?
10. Who is outside the city and not permitted to enter?
11. Who forfeited their right to the tree of life and their entrance into the kingdom?
12. When is our eternal destiny secure?
13. In Philippians 3, did Paul consider himself to have attained?
14. In 1 Corinthians 9. Why did Paul make his body his slave, what was he concerned about?
15. Who qualified us to share in the inheritance of His holy people?
16. In Matthew 24, what did Jesus refer to as the good news that must be proclaim unto all nations?
17. In 2 Thessalonians 1, why was Paul boasting to other churches about the church in Thessalonica?
18. How should we run the race set before us?
19. What is our eternal destiny dependent on?

Chapter 13

He Will Never Forsake Us

Just the other night I was continuing this study by considering another verse used to support the teaching of once save, always saved. This verse was from Hebrews 13:5. "Be free from the love of money, content with such things as you have, for he has said, 'I will in no way leave you, neither will I in any way forsake you.'" The last part of this passage is a quote from Deuteronomy 31:8.

As I considered this passage in Hebrews, I was prompted to turn to the source of the quote in Deuteronomy. In that passage, Moses is encouraging the children of Israel as they prepare to enter the promised land and drive out the nations that lived there saying, "Be strong and courageous. Do not be afraid or terrified because of them, for the LORD your God goes with you; he will never leave you nor forsake you" (NIV).

I continued to read from verse eight down to verse sixteen to get a sense of the context. It was then that I was shocked as I read, "And the LORD said to Moses: 'You are going to rest with your ancestors, and these people will soon prostitute themselves to the foreign gods of the land they are entering. They will forsake me and break the covenant I made with them.

"And in that day I will become angry with them and forsake them; I will hide my face from them, and they will be destroyed. Many disasters and calamities will come on them, and in that day they will ask, "Have not these disasters come on us because our God is not with us?" And I will certainly

125

hide my face in that day because of all their wickedness in turning to other gods'" (Deuteronomy 31:16-18, NIV).

How could this be? In verse eight, God promises He will never forsake His people. Then in verse seventeen, God says He will forsake them. I believe the scriptures are true. I also believe it is not possible for God to lie (Hebrews 6:18).

I checked with Strong's Concordance to make sure that the words translated in these verses were both from the same Hebrew word. They were. They were both from word #5800, azab.

So, no matter how you translate the word azab, in verse eight God says He will not do this to His people and in verse seventeen He says He will do this to His people. Therefore what God means when He says He will not forsake us is something different then I and most Christians believe He means.

It becomes clear from the passages in this chapter that God is not giving His people a license to live any way they desire because of His promise never to forsake them. No, He is promising to remain faithful to them as long as they remain faithful to Him.

If God's people forsake Him, God is no longer bound to His commitment not to forsake them. I could almost hear cries of objection to this interpretation from my old religious self, saying, "This was from the old covenant, it is different under the freedom of the new covenant."

I was reminded, to have confidence that any understanding of scripture is accurate, it must be true to the context of the specific passages and true to the full council of God. As I considered this, I was prompted to turn to John 15 and consider the words of Jesus as He speaks to His disciples.

Jesus said, "I am the true vine, and my Father is the farmer. Every branch in me that doesn't bear fruit, he takes away. Every branch that bears fruit, he prunes, that it may bear more fruit. You are already pruned clean because of the word which I have spoken to you.

"Remain in me, and I in you. As the branch can't bear fruit by itself unless it remains in the vine, so neither can you, unless you remain in me. I am the vine. You are the branches.

"He who remains in me and I in him bears much fruit, for apart from me you can do nothing. If a man doesn't remain in me, he is thrown out as a branch and is withered; and they gather them, throw them into the fire, and they are burned" (John 15:1-6).

I began to realize, the covenants may have changed, but God has not. "They will forsake me and break the covenant I made with them. And in that day I will become angry with them and forsake them." "Every branch in me that doesn't bear fruit, he takes away." And again, "If a man doesn't remain in me, he is thrown out as a branch and is withered; and they gather them, throw them into the fire, and they are burned."

When Jesus tells His disciples, "Remain in me, and I in you," He is giving His disciples notice that His abiding, His continuing to remain in them, is contingent on their continuing to remain in Him. In another translation, this verse is rendered as, "Continue in me and I will be continually in you" (John 15:4, TFLV).

Jesus testifies to His disciples, "Every branch in me that doesn't bear fruit, he takes away," And again, "If a man doesn't remain in me, he is thrown out as a branch and is withered; and they gather them, throw them into the fire, and they are burned." His commitment to abide in us is contingent on our abiding in Him.

Paul reaffirms this in his letter to the church in Rome. He writes to the believers, "If some of the branches were broken off, and you, being a wild olive, were grafted in among them and became partaker with them of the root and of the richness of the olive tree, don't boast over the branches. But if you boast, it is not you who support the root, but the root supports you.

"You will say then, 'Branches were broken off, that I might be grafted in.' True; by their unbelief they were broken off, and you stand by your faith. Don't be conceited, but fear; for if God didn't spare the natural branches, neither will he spare you.

"See then the goodness and severity of God. Toward those who fell, severity; but toward you, goodness, if you continue in his goodness; otherwise you also will be cut off" (Romans 11:17-22).

Whenever we see the word "if" used, we need to be aware that the one thing being mentioned is contingent on the other thing being mentioned. If you continue faithful, you will not be cut off. However, if you do not continue faithful, you will be cut off.

Paul also warns the believers in Corinth. "If any man defile the temple of God, him shall God destroy; for the temple of God is holy, which temple ye are" (I Corinthians 3:17, KJV).

And again, in 1 Corinthians 6:19-20 Paul exhorts the believers saying, "Or don't you know that your body is a temple of the Holy Spirit who is in you, whom you have from God? You are not your own, for you were bought with a price. Therefore glorify God in your body and in your spirit, which are God's.

And finally, "What agreement is there between the temple of God and idols? For we are the temple of the living God. As God has said: 'I will live with them and walk among them, and I will be their God, and they will be, my people'" (2 Corinthians 6:16).

Peter reminds the believers that God has given us everything we need to live holy, godly lives. "His divine power has given us everything we need for a godly life through our knowledge of him who called us by his own glory and goodness. Through these he has given us his very great and precious promises, so that through them you may participate in the divine nature, having escaped the corruption in the world caused by evil desires" (2 Peter 1:3-4).

God, by virtue of His power working in us through the indwelling Holy Spirit, has given us everything we need to live holy lives. By our death with Christ through our baptism by the Holy Spirit into Christ, we have been liberated, set free

Walking in the Light

from bondage to sin. In Christ, sin no longer has dominion over us. We have been set free to walk by the Spirit, serving God in newness of life.

Now if a believer sins, it is not because he was forced to, it is because he has chosen to. As a born-again believer, he has been set free from the bondage and dominion of sin and has been given everything required to live a holy, godly life while still in the midst of this crooked, perverse world.

James explains this to us saying, "Let no man say when he is tempted, "I am tempted by God," for God can't be tempted by evil, and he himself tempts no one. But each one is tempted when he is drawn away by his own lust and enticed. Then the lust, when it has conceived, bears sin. The sin, when it is full grown, produces death" (James 1:13-15).

Many Christians consider sin in their lives as a small thing, something that is not serious. I have heard many versions of whitewashing the issue. Some will say, "All of my sins have been forgiven, past, present and future, so I am covered." Or, "Sure, I sin continually, many times every day, but I am okay. Look at Paul's testimony in Romans chapter seven about his constant struggle with sin as a believer. He says in chapter seven that he is enslaved to sin, that he has no power to do the good he wants to do, and that he practices the evil he does not want to do."

Other professing Christians say, "When God looks at me, He doesn't see me, He sees Jesus." Yet another has told me, "God is pleased with me because Jesus is in me, and He is pleased with Jesus. It does not matter what I do, God is still pleased with me."

Finally, a pastor and a teacher at a church in our area said, "It is impossible for a believer, a Christian, to go even one minute without sinning, because we as born-again believers are still sinners by nature. Everything we do is sin."

Among passages that come to mind when I hear statements like these are those from the book of Jeremiah and from Paul in his letter to Timothy. In Jeremiah we read, "An astonishing and horrible thing has happened in the land. The prophets prophesy falsely, and the priests rule by their own authority; and my people love to have it so. What will you do in the end of it?"

Continuing in the next chapter we read, "From the least to the greatest, all are greedy for gain; prophets and priests alike, all practice deceit. They dress the wound of my people as though it were not serious. 'Peace, peace,' they say, when there is no peace. Are they ashamed of their detestable conduct? No, they have no shame at all; they do not even know how to blush. So they will fall among the fallen; they will be brought down when I punish them,' say the Lord" (Jeremiah 5:30-31, 6:13-15, NIV).

Paul writes to Timothy about these fleshly minded Christians. "Having a form of godliness, but denying the power thereof: from such turn away" (2 Timothy 3:5, KJV). I can not conceive of a more fitting description of professing Christians that have an appearance of religion, a form of godliness, but that deny the power of God that He gives to every born-again believer to live godly, holy lives. God is adamant in His instruction, "From such turn away."

Paul addresses this matter in his letter to the Corinthians. "It is actually reported that there is sexual immorality among you, and of a kind that even pagans do not tolerate: A man is sleeping with his father's wife. And you are proud! Shouldn't you rather have gone into mourning and have put out of your fellowship the man who has been doing this?

"Your boasting is not good. Don't you know that a little yeast leavens the whole batch of dough? Get rid of the old yeast, so that you may be a new unleavened batch—as you really are. For Christ, our Passover lamb, has been sacrificed. Therefore let us keep the Festival, not with the old bread leavened with malice and wickedness, but with the unleavened bread of sincerity and truth.

"I wrote to you in my letter not to associate with sexually immoral people— not at all meaning the people of this world who are immoral, or the greedy and swindlers, or idolaters. In that case you would have to leave this world. But

Walking in the Light

now I am writing to you that you must not associate with anyone who claims to be a brother or sister but is sexually immoral or greedy, an idolater or slanderer, a drunkard or swindler. Do not even eat with such people.

"What business is it of mine to judge those outside the church? Are you not to judge those inside? God will judge those outside. "Expel the wicked person from among you" (1 Corinthians 5:1-2, 6-13, NIV).

God does not take sin among His people lightly, or as a small thing. Paul warns us, "Walk by the Spirit, and you will not gratify the desires of the flesh. For the flesh desires what is contrary to the Spirit, and the Spirit what is contrary to the flesh. They are in conflict with each other, so that you are not to do whatever you want. But if you are led by the Spirit, you are not under the law.

"The acts of the flesh are obvious: sexual immorality, impurity and debauchery; idolatry and witchcraft; hatred, discord, jealousy, fits of rage, selfish ambition, dissensions, factions and envy; drunkenness, orgies, and the like. I warn you, as I did before, that those who live like this will not inherit the kingdom of God.

"But the fruit of the Spirit is love, joy, peace, forbearance, kindness, goodness, faithfulness, gentleness and self-control. Against such things there is no law. Those who belong to Christ Jesus have crucified the flesh with its passions and desires. Since we live by the Spirit, let us keep in step with the Spirit" (Galatians 5:16-25).

The apostle John testifies, "Then I saw a new heaven and a new earth; for the first heaven and the first earth passed away, and there is no longer any sea. And I saw the holy city, new Jerusalem, coming down out of heaven from God, prepared as a bride adorned for her husband.

"And I heard a loud voice from the throne, saying, 'Behold, the tabernacle of God is among the people, and He will dwell among them, and they shall be His people, and God Himself will be among them, and He will wipe away every tear from their eyes; and there will no longer be any death; there will no longer be any mourning, or crying, or pain; the first things have passed away.'

"And He who sits on the throne said, 'Behold, I am making all things new.' And He said, 'Write, for these words are faithful and true.' Then He said to me, 'It is done. I am the Alpha and the Omega, the beginning and the end. I will give water to the one who thirsts from the spring of the water of life, without cost. The one who overcomes will inherit these things, and I will be his God and he will be My son.

"'But for the cowardly, and unbelieving, and abominable, and murderers, and sexually immoral persons, and sorcerers, and idolaters, and all liars, their part will be in the lake that burns with fire and brimstone, which is the second death'" (Revelation 21:1-8).

At the end of the last book of the Bible, Jesus announces, "Blessed are those who wash their robes, so that they will have the right to the tree of life, and may enter the city by the gates. Outside are the dogs, the sorcerers, the sexually immoral persons, the murderers, the idolaters, and everyone who loves and practices lying" (Revelation 22:14-15).

It becomes evident that if we forsake God, He will forsake us. A covenant is a legal contract. When one party to that contract violates the terms of the contract, the other party is released from their obligations under that contract.

God promises He will never break His covenant with us. He promises He will keep His word. His word will not return to Him void. It will accomplish exactly what He sent it to do. The righteous will be rewarded according to His word. The evildoers will also be rewarded according to His word.

It seems very clear from these passages that people who have made a practice of sinning, who have made a practice of walking according to the flesh, will not be found worthy of the kingdom. They will not be permitted to enter the city or to have access to the tree of life.

According to these verses, the destiny of those that practice such things will be outside the city or in the lake of fire, the second death. I do not know which would apply in any specific case, perhaps it will depend on the severity of their rebellion.

Chapter 13 Discussion Questions:
He Will Never Forsake Us

1. What passage in the old testament is Hebrews 13:5 quoted from?
2. In Deuteronomy 31:16-17, what does God say He will do if His people forsake Him?
3. When God says He will never forsake His people, what does He mean?
4. In John 15:6, what does Jesus say will happen to someone that does not remain in Him?
5. What is Jesus' abiding, remaining in us, contingent upon?
6. In Romans 11:20-21, what does Paul tell us to fear?
7. In Jeremiah 6:13-15, how do the prophets and the priests treat the wound of God's people as though it was not serious?
8. What is meant by "having a form of godliness, but denying the power thereof?
9. What is meant by "a little yeast leavens the whole batch?
10. Who will not be found worthy of the kingdom?
11. Who will not enter the city, new Jerusalem, or have access to the tree of life?

Chapter 14

Take Heed Lest You Fall

In this chapter we want to review some of the many warnings that we find throughout the scriptures concerning the constant danger of falling short of what God has prepared for us as His people. In reviewing these many warnings, we want to consider how they might apply to those of us who are truly born-again believers.

Many professing Christians believe that it is not possible for a genuine, born-again believer to fall away from the living God. They believe that because God started this salvation process, it is His responsibility to see that it is completed, and that He will do that regardless of our unfaithfulness.

Many believe that it is not possible for a genuine Christian to fail to finish the course that God has set him on. They claim that if a professing Christian falls away, that person could not possibly have been a real Christian. His falling away is in fact proof that he was not a true Christian.

Again, our desire is to know the truth. To come to a better understanding of the truth, we must be willing to allow the scriptures to interpret the scriptures. We must humble ourselves and be willing to drop all our preconceptions and allow the Holy Spirit to teach us.

Let us begin by considering Hebrews 10:26-39. "If we deliberately keep on sinning after we have received the knowledge of the truth, no sacrifice for sins is left, but only a fearful expectation of judgment and of raging fire that will consume the enemies of God. Anyone who rejected the law of

Walking in the Light

Moses died without mercy on the testimony of two or three witnesses.

"How much more severely do you think someone deserves to be punished who has trampled the Son of God underfoot, who has treated as an unholy thing the blood of the covenant that sanctified them, and who has insulted the Spirit of grace? For we know him who said, 'It is mine to avenge; I will repay,' and again, 'The Lord will judge his people.' It is a dreadful thing to fall into the hands of the living God.

"Remember those earlier days after you had received the light, when you endured in a great conflict full of suffering. Sometimes you were publicly exposed to insult and persecution; at other times you stood side by side with those who were so treated. You suffered along with those in prison and joyfully accepted the confiscation of your property, because you knew that you yourselves had better and lasting possessions. So do not throw away your confidence; it will be richly rewarded.

"You need to persevere so that when you have done the will of God, you will receive what he has promised. For, 'In just a little while, he who is coming will come and will not delay.' And, 'But, my righteous one will live by faith. And I take no pleasure in the one who shrinks back.' But we do not belong to those who shrink back and are destroyed, but to those who have faith and are saved."

In this passage the writer of Hebrews speaks of one that had received the knowledge of the truth, and afterward has deliberately continued to sin. For such a person, there remains no sacrifice for sins, but a terrifying expectation of judgment. This person has insulted the Spirit of grace, regarded as profane the blood of the covenant by which he was sanctified.

We are encouraged not to be like this one, because we have a better and enduring possession, better than the one under the first covenant, better than under the law of Moses. We are encouraged not to throw away our confidence, which has a great reward.

Jon von Ernst

We are encouraged to endure to the end, so that after we have done God's will, we may inherit the promises. We are further encouraged by being reminded that Christ's return will be very soon, and that we need to continue to walk by faith. Christ abides in us as our righteousness, if we continue in faithful obedience to the Spirit's leading, if we continue to walk by faith, enduring to the end.

We are warned again that His righteous one must not draw back. If he does, God will have no pleasure in him. In fact, he goes on to say that the one that draws back will be destroyed, but those that continue faithful to the end will obtain life.

God speaks in the book of Ezekiel of His displeasure with those who draw back, turning away from God and His righteousness. "If I tell a righteous person that they will surely live, but then they trust in their righteousness and do evil, none of the righteous things that person has done will be remembered; they will die for the evil they have done.

"And if I say to a wicked person, 'You will surely die,' but they then turn away from their sin and do what is just and right— if they give back what they took in pledge for a loan, return what they have stolen, follow the decrees that give life, and do no evil—that person will surely live; they will not die. None of the sins that person has committed will be remembered against them. They have done what is just and right; they will surely live.

"Yet your people say, 'The way of the Lord is not just.' But it is their way that is not just. If a righteous person turns from their righteousness and does evil, they will die for it. And if a wicked person turns away from their wickedness and does what is just and right, they will live by doing so. Yet you Israelites say, 'The way of the Lord is not just.' But I will judge each of you according to your own ways" (Ezekiel 33:13-20, NIV).

There are many professing Christians that seem to believe that God is bound to His promises, but they are not bound to anything, that they are under no obligation to do anything. They seem to believe that the Christian life is just a matter of

Walking in the Light

faith and faith alone. As long as you believe you believe, you are okay.

According to many of them, there is no place for works in our becoming saved or in our remaining secure in that salvation. Apparently, it is all of faith, and none of works. We couldn't earn it, and we can't lose it.

This is reminiscent of the husband who believes that his wife is bound to be faithful to him because of the vows that she made when they were married. However, this husband seems to sense no obligation to any vows he may have made to his wife. Therefore, the husband envisions himself as one that is free to be faithful or not to be faithful, depending on whatever he finds most pleasing at the moment.

A false understanding of the truth, believing a lie, can produce a false sense of security. It can produce a sense of arrogance while walking in error. This arrogance, this pride, seems to grow to a pinnacle of folly just before the fall. Indeed, pride comes before the fall, and behold how great that fall will be!

Let us continue by turning to the second letter of Peter. "But there were also false prophets among the people, just as there will be false teachers among you. They will secretly introduce destructive heresies, even denying the sovereign Lord who bought them—bringing swift destruction on themselves.

"Many will follow their depraved conduct and will bring the way of truth into disrepute. In their greed these teachers will exploit you with fabricated stories. Their condemnation has long been hanging over them, and their destruction has not been sleeping. . . These people are springs without water and mists driven by a storm.

"Blackest darkness is reserved for them. For they mouth empty, boastful words and, by appealing to the lustful desires of the flesh, they entice people who are just escaping from those who live in error. They promise them freedom, while they themselves are slaves of depravity—for 'people are slaves to whatever has mastered them.'

"If they have escaped the corruption of the world by knowing our Lord and Savior Jesus Christ and are again entangled in it and are overcome, they are worse off at the end than they were at the beginning. It would have been better for them not to have known the way of righteousness, than to have known it and then to turn their backs on the sacred command that was passed on to them" (2 Peter 2:1-3, 17-21, NIV).

In this passage, Peter speaks of people who had escaped the world's impurity through the knowledge of our Lord and Savior Jesus Christ, who are again entangled with the sins of the world and are defeated. The last state for them is worse than the first. After having been saved, knowing Jesus as Lord and Savior, they turned back, loving the world and the things of the world. They turned back having eyes full of adultery, and always looking for sin, seducing unstable people.

These people weren't just born-again Christians, they were teachers, they were prophets. They began to err from the truth by secretly bringing in destructive heresies, even denying the Master who bought them. They were bold arrogant people. They led many away because of their unrestrained ways. Because of them the way of truth is blasphemed. It would have been better for them not to have known the way of righteousness than, after knowing it, to turn back from the holy commandments delivered to them.

In his letters to the Colossians and to Philemon, Paul sends greetings from some of the co-workers that were the closest to him. "Luke the beloved physician and Demas greet you" (Colossioans 4:14). "Epaphras, my fellow prisoner in Christ Jesus, greets you, as do Mark, Aristarchus, Demas, and Luke, my fellow workers" (Philemon 23-24).

A little later Paul writes to Timothy concerning Demas. "Be diligent to come to me soon, for Demas left me, having loved this present world, and went to Thessalonica; Crescens to Galatia; and Titus to Dalmatia. Only Luke is with me. Take Mark, and bring him with you, for he is useful to me for service." (2 Timothy 4:9-11). It seems clear that Demas was in fact a genuine Christian before he fell away.

Walking in the Light

Paul warns the believers in Romans 11, "But if some of the branches were broken off, and you, being a wild olive, were grafted in among them and became partaker with them of the rich root of the olive tree, do not be arrogant toward the branches; but if you are arrogant, remember that it is not you who supports the root, but the root supports you. You will say then, 'Branches were broken off so that I might be grafted in.' Quite right, they were broken off for their unbelief, but you stand by your faith. Do not be conceited, but fear; for if God did not spare the natural branches, He will not spare you, either. See then the kindness and severity of God: to those who fell, severity, but to you, God's kindness, if you continue in His kindness; for otherwise you too will be cut off" (Romans 11:17-22, NASB).

Paul has addressed this letter "To all who are in Rome, beloved of God, called to be saints." Clearly he is speaking to the Christians in the church in Rome. He is speaking to believers that have been grafted in and have become part of the body of Christ. He warns them not to be arrogant, but to fear.

When he says not to be arrogant, he seems to be referring to those that believe it is not possible for themselves to be cut off. He reminds them that they stand by faith and that those natural branches that have been cut off were cutoff because of unbelief.

He charges them to consider God's kindness and severity. Severity towards those that have fallen, but kindness toward you, if you remain in His kindness. Otherwise they, the Christians in Rome, would also would be cut off.

It is amazing how God's word, when taken at face value, can cause us to tremble! Perhaps this is what Paul was referring to when he wrote to the believers in the church in Philippians 2:12, "So then, my beloved, even as you have always obeyed, not only in my presence, but now much more in my absence, work out your own salvation with fear and trembling."

Jon von Ernst

The writer of Hebrews addresses those he was writing to saying, "Therefore, holy brothers, partakers of a heavenly calling, consider the Apostle and High Priest of our confession: Jesus, who was faithful to him who appointed him, as also Moses was in all his house. . . But Christ is faithful as a Son over his house. We are his house, if we hold fast our confidence and the glorying of our hope firm to the end.

"Beware, brothers, lest perhaps there might be in any one of you an evil heart of unbelief, in falling away from the living God; but exhort one another day by day, so long as it is called "today", lest any one of you be hardened by the deceitfulness of sin. For we have become partakers of Christ, if we hold the beginning of our confidence firm to the end, while it is said, 'Today if you will hear His voice, don't harden your hearts, as in the rebellion.'

"For who, when they heard, rebelled? Wasn't it all those who came out of Egypt led by Moses? With whom was he displeased forty years? Wasn't it with those who sinned, whose bodies fell in the wilderness? To whom did he swear that they wouldn't enter into his rest, but to those who were disobedient? We see that they weren't able to enter in because of unbelief.

"Let's fear therefore, lest perhaps anyone of you should seem to have come short of a promise of entering into his rest" (Hebrews 3:1, 6, 12-19, 4:1).

The writer is speaking to Christians, addressing them as holy brothers, partakers of a heavenly calling. He is encouraging them to remain steadfast in the faith, holding their confidence firm to the end. He is warning them about the danger of falling away from God because of an evil heart of unbelief. This is why it is necessary that we encourage each other daily, as long as it is called 'today'.

He reminds them that we have become partakers of Christ, if we hold firm to the end. Those that rebelled were disobedient, their hearts were hardened. Therefore they were unable to enter into His rest.

Walking in the Light

He warns the believers that, in the same way, their hearts could become hardened by the deceitfulness of sin. These believers are told to fear, lest any of them should come short of the promise of entering into His rest. Because of the deceitfulness of sin, believers hearts are in danger of being hardened and falling away from the living God.

Jesus said, "I tell you that many will come from the east and the west, and will sit down with Abraham, Isaac, and Jacob in the Kingdom of Heaven, but the children of the Kingdom will be thrown out into the outer darkness. There will be weeping and gnashing of teeth" (Matthew 8:11-12).

I believe that when Jesus uses the term "the children of the kingdom," He is referring to those that are trusting in their godly heritage, their religious background or their religious training. Because of this background according to the flesh, these people are very confident that they will be welcomed into the kingdom of God with open arms. These people are in for a very rude awakening when they find themselves thrown out into the shady area of darkness outside of the kingdom. There will be much weeping and gnashing of teeth as they realize that they had been so badly deceived.

Jesus told a parable of a king that said to his servants, "'The wedding is ready, but those who were invited weren't worthy. Go therefore to the intersections of the highways, and as many as you may find, invite to the wedding feast.' Those servants went out into the highways and gathered together as many as they found, both bad and good. The wedding was filled with guests.

"But when the king came in to see the guests, he saw there a man who didn't have on wedding clothing, and he said to him, 'Friend, how did you come in here not wearing wedding clothing?' He was speechless.

"Then the king said to the servants, 'Bind him hand and foot, take him away, and throw him into the outer darkness. That is where the weeping and grinding of teeth will be.' For many are called, but few chosen" (Matthew 22:8-14).

Again Jesus taught using a parable, "He also who had received the one talent came and said, 'Lord, I knew you that you are a hard man, reaping where you didn't sow, and gathering where you didn't scatter. I was afraid, and went away and hid your talent in the earth. Behold, you have what is yours.'

"But his lord answered him, 'You wicked and slothful servant. You knew that I reap where I didn't sow, and gather where I didn't scatter. You ought therefore to have deposited my money with the bankers, and at my coming I should have received back my own with interest. Take away therefore the talent from him and give it to him who has the ten talents.

"For to everyone who has will be given, and he will have abundance, but from him who doesn't have, even that which he has will be taken away. Throw out the unprofitable servant into the outer darkness, where there will be weeping and gnashing of teeth'" (Matthew 25:24-30).

Jesus makes it clear that unfaithful believers will not be found worthy to enter into the kingdom of God, but will be cast out into outer darkness, where there will be weeping and gnashing of teeth. Entrance into the holy city, new Jerusalem, being denied to them, at best they may find themselves outside the city, away from the presence of God, in the outer darkness where the nations will be (Revelation 21:8, 23-27, 22:14-15).

Chapter 14 Discussion Questions:
Take Heed Lest You Fall

1. What danger are many passages throughout scripture warning us about?
2. Is the passage in Hebrews 10:26-39 speaking about a genuine Christian? How do you know?
3. Why did the believers that this passage was written to joyfully accept the confiscation of their possessions?
4. Why are we encouraged to endure to the end?

Walking in the Light

5. What happens to those that do not endure to the end but shrink back?
6. What does God say, in the book of Ezekiel, will happen to a righteous person that trusts in their righteousness and does evil?
7. What can believing false teaching, believing a lie, produce?
8. Was the person referred to in 2 Peter chapter 2 a genuine Christian? How do you know?
9. Paul states that Demas left him, having loved this present world. Was Demas a genuine Christian?
10. In Romans 11, Paul writes to believers saying, "You stand by your faith. Do not be conceited, but fear; for if God did not spare the natural branches, He will not spare you, either." Was he speaking to genuine Christians?
11. What did Paul say would happen to a believer if they did not continue in God's kindness?
12. Who does Paul tell not to be arrogant, but to fear?
13. What should cause a believer to tremble?
14. In Hebrews chapter 3, the believers are warned that something could cause their hearts to be hardened. What was he warning them about?
15. Who did Jesus refer to as "the children of the kingdom"?
16. What happened to the 'wicked and slothful servant' that was afraid to use the talent that his lord had given to him?
17. What will be the eternal destiny of unfaithful believers?

Chapter 15

Worthy of the Kingdom

It seems that the real joy of many professing Christians today is the thought of leaving this world and going to heaven when they die or are raptured, and to be in God's heavenly kingdom forever. In this chapter, we will endeavor to determine if this joy is based firmly on the truth as revealed in scripture or if it is merely based on wishful thinking and the doctrines of man.

Let's start by reading what Jesus tells us in Matthew 7:21-23, "Not everyone who says to Me, 'Lord, Lord!' will enter the kingdom of heaven, but only the one who does the will of My Father in heaven. On that day many will say to Me, 'Lord, Lord, didn't we prophesy in Your name, drive out demons in Your name, and do many miracles in Your name?' Then I will announce to them, 'I never knew you! Depart from Me, you lawbreakers!'" (HCSB).

On that day, the day of judgment, everyone will stand before the Lord to give an account of the things that they did while living in their physical bodies during their time on this earth. "For we must all appear before judgment seat of Christ, so that each may be repaid for what he has done in the body, whether good or bad" (2 Corinthians 5:10).

On that day, each will be hoping that in some way they might be found to be worthy of the kingdom of heaven. Many of those will be ones that never believed that there was a heaven or a hell, and lived accordingly, not expecting to ever have to give an account for the things they did while in their physical bodies.

Walking in the Light

Others may have believed there was a heaven and a hell, but were confident that, because they professed to be Christians, they would not be judged, but instead would be ushered directly into the kingdom of heaven. Their confidence may have been based on things they had said or done, or on the assurances that were given to them by their parents or by various religious leaders.

They may have said a prayer of repentance, feeling sorry for their sins and even asked Jesus to come into their hearts. They may have joined a church, perhaps even became a deacon or a Sunday school teacher. Maybe they attended a seminary or a Bible college and became a pastor, music leader, missionary, or some other Christian worker.

Perhaps they started churches, schools or hospitals and cast out demons and healed the sick. Maybe they just gave all they had to the poor or gave their bodies to be burned (1 Corinthians 13:3). Surely, God would gladly receive them into His heavenly kingdom.

What a blessing of peace and comfort these people experienced during their lifetimes resting on the promises of God. Knowing that God is love. God is rich in mercy. His grace, abundant and free, is sufficient for all our needs. His forgiveness is freely available to all who believe. These are all such wonderful truths found in scripture. And of course, God will surely receive us into His heavenly kingdom. Right?

Well, let's look at that passage from Matthew chapter seven once again. It tells us that not everyone who claims to be a Christian, not everyone who calls Jesus 'Lord' will enter into the kingdom of heaven. No, only the one who does the will of the Father will enter.

What? How can this be? Our God is loving and kind, rich in mercy, forgiving, with grace abounding to all who believe.

The ones that were being denied entrance into the kingdom tried to make their case before the judge, Christ Jesus our Lord. They said to Him, "Lord, Lord, didn't we do many great things in Your name? Didn't we prophecy in Your name? Didn't we drive out demons in Your name? Didn't we work many miracles in Your name?"

They will stand there in total shock and disbelief as Jesus announces to them, "I never knew you! Depart from Me, you lawbreakers!"

In their agonized response they may cry out to Jesus, "We prayed to you. We read the Bible. We even memorized dozens of verses. We faithfully attended church. How can you say that you never knew us? We were assured that we were saved and could never lose our salvation. We were assured that you would never leave us or forsake us.

"Didn't we confess you before men? Don't you remember our confirmation confession? What about the confession we made when we were baptized? How can you call us lawbreakers? How can you claim that you never knew us?"

What did Jesus mean when He called them lawbreakers? To understand what Jesus was telling them, we need to look to the scriptures. The apostle John explains, "Everyone who commits sin also breaks the law; sin is the breaking of the law" (1 John 3:4, HCSB)

Paul elaborates on this idea saying, "Now the deeds of the flesh are obvious, which are: adultery, sexual immorality, uncleanness, lustfulness, idolatry, sorcery, hatred, strife, jealousies, outbursts of anger, rivalries, divisions, heresies, envy, murders, drunkenness, orgies, and things like these; of which I forewarn you, even as I also forewarned you, that those who practice such things will not inherit God's Kingdom" (Galatians 5:19-21).

"So I say this, and affirm in the Lord, that you are to no longer walk just as the Gentiles also walk, in the futility of their minds, being darkened in their understanding, excluded from the life of God because of the ignorance that is in them, because of the hardness of their heart; and they, having become callous, have given themselves up to indecent behavior for the practice of every kind of impurity with greediness. But you did not learn Christ in this way, if indeed you have heard Him and have been taught in Him, just as truth is in Jesus, that, in reference to your former way of life, you are to rid yourselves of the old self, which is being corrupted in accordance with the lusts of deceit, and that you are to be renewed in the spirit of your minds, and to put on the new self, which in the likeness of God has been created in righteousness and holiness of the truth." (Ephesians 4:17-24, NASB).

Paul, writing to Christians, warns, "I am afraid that on this next visit my God will humble me along with you and I will mourn for many who have been living in sin and have not repented of their impure relationships: of engaging in sex outside of marriage and of the unholy sexual behavior which they have been practicing" (2 Corinthians 12:20-21 TFL).

The apostles understood that we are in a spiritual battle. They understood that the flesh is warring against the Spirit, and the Spirit is warring against the flesh. Therefore, they repeatedly warned believers to be careful about how they lived.

They begged them, they implored them, and prayed for them that they would walk worthily of God, that they would be counted worthy to enter His kingdom. They exhorted them that they would not sin, that they would not love the world.

I "beg you to walk worthily of the calling with which you were called" (Ephesians 4:1). We "don't cease praying and making requests for you, that you may be filled with the knowledge of his will in all spiritual wisdom and understanding, that you may walk worthily of the Lord" (Colossians 1:9).

We "implored every one of you, as a father does his own children, to the end that you should walk worthily of God, who calls you into his own Kingdom and glory" (1 Thessalonians 2:12). "Your perseverance and faith in all your persecutions and in the afflictions which you endure . . . is an obvious sign of the righteous judgment of God, to the end that you may be counted worthy of God's Kingdom, for which you also suffer" (2 Thessalonians 1:4-5).

John writes, "My little children, I am writing these things to you so that you may not sin. And if anyone sins, we have an Advocate with the Father, Jesus Christ the righteous; and He Himself is the propitiation for our sins; and not for ours only, but also for the sins of the whole world.

"By this we know that we have come to know Him, if we keep His commandments. The one who says, "I have come to know Him," and does not keep His commandments, is a liar, and the truth is not in him; but whoever follows His word, in him the love of God has truly been perfected. By this we know that we are in Him: the one who says that he remains in Him ought, himself also, walk just as He (Jesus) walked" (1 John 2:1-6, NASB).

"Don't love the world or the things that are in the world. If anyone loves the world, the Father's love isn't in him. For all that is in the world, the lust of the flesh, the lust of the eyes, and the pride of life, isn't the Father's, but is the world's. The world is passing away with its lusts, but he who does God's will remains forever" (1 John 2:15-17).

Peter assures us, "His divine power has given us everything required for life and godliness through the knowledge of Him who called us by His own glory and goodness. By these He has given us very great and precious promises, so that through them you may share in the divine nature, escaping the corruption that is in the world because of evil desires. For this very reason, make every effort to supplement your faith with goodness, goodness with knowledge, knowledge with self-control, self-control with endurance, endurance with godliness, godliness with brotherly affection, and brotherly affection with love.

"For if these qualities are yours and are increasing, they will keep you from being useless or unfruitful in the knowledge of our Lord Jesus Christ. The person who lacks these things is blind and shortsighted and has forgotten the cleansing from his past sins. Therefore, brothers, make every effort to confirm your calling and election, because if you do these things you will never stumble. For in this way, entry into the eternal kingdom of our Lord and Savior Jesus Christ will be richly supplied to you." (2 Peter 1:3-11, HCSB).

Jesus and the apostles warned the believers to be careful not to be led astray. Jesus answered the Sadducees that were testing Him saying, "You are deceived, because you don't know the Scriptures or the power of God" (Matthew 22:29).

When we don't know the scriptures, we are easily deceived. The indwelling Holy Spirit teaches the born-again believer all things. This teaching by the Spirit of Christ within us protects us from the deception of false teachers. Professing Christians that do not know the scriptures and are not being taught by the indwelling Holy Spirit will be easily deceived.

John reminds us, "These things I have written to you concerning those who are trying to deceive you. And as for you, the anointing which you received from Him remains in you, and you have no need for anyone to teach you; but as His anointing teaches you about all things, and is true and is not a lie, and just as it has taught you, you remain in Him.

"Now, little children, remain in Him, so that when He appears, we may have confidence and not draw back from Him in shame at His coming. If you know that He is righteous, you know that everyone who practices righteousness also has been born of Him" (1 John 2:26-29, NASB).

The merely natural man, using his natural intellect, cannot discern the truths hidden in the scriptures. Therefore the merely natural man will be easily deceived and will be carried to and fro by every wind of doctrine. He will have itching ears and will embrace one doctrine of man after another. Only the Holy Spirit can reveal these truths to us. We must be born of the Spirit. We must be taught by the Holy Spirit, only then can we truly understand the scriptures and know the power of God.

John reminds us, "We know that when He appears, we will be like Him, because we will see Him just as He is. And everyone who has this hope set on Him purifies himself, just as He is pure.

"Everyone who practices sin also practices lawlessness; and sin is lawlessness. You know that He appeared in order to take away sins; and in Him there is no sin. No one who remains in Him sins continually; no one who sins continually has seen Him or knows Him." (1 John 3:2-6, NASB).

As we are led by the indwelling Spirit, He directs us and reveals to us areas in our lives that are not pleasing to God. The Spirit then empowers us to have the courage to repent and humble ourselves and give our Lord Jesus Christ permission to do whatever is necessary in our lives to purify ourselves from whatever it is in our hearts that is not pleasing to Him. The indwelling Spirit then empowers us to obey His leading as He directs us as to whatever we must do to put off the old man and put on the new man that has been renewed in Christ.

John continues, "Little children, make sure no one deceives you; the one who practices righteousness is righteous, just as He is righteous; the one who practices sin is of the devil; for the devil has been sinning from the beginning. The Son of God appeared for this purpose, to destroy the works of the devil" (1 John 3:7-8, NASB).

"We know love by this, that He laid down His life for us; and we ought to lay down our lives for the brothers and sisters. But whoever has worldly goods and sees his brother or sister in need, and closes his heart against him, how does the love of God remain in him? Little children, let's not love with word or with tongue, but in deed and truth. . . This is His commandment, that we believe in the name of His Son Jesus Christ, and love one another, just as He commanded us. The one who keeps His commandments remains in Him, and He in him. We know by this that He remains in us, by the Spirit whom He has given us" (1 John 3:16-18, 23-24, NASB).

Paul reveals to believers his heart toward the things of the flesh and his heart toward the things of the Spirit. He explains how the things he values in his heart determine how he lives his life.

"For we are the true circumcision, who worship in the Spirit of God and take pride in Christ Jesus, and put no confidence in the flesh, although I myself could boast as having confidence even in the flesh. If anyone else thinks

Walking in the Light

he is confident in the flesh, I have more reason: circumcised the eighth day, of the nation of Israel, of the tribe of Benjamin, a Hebrew of Hebrews; as to the Law, a Pharisee; as to zeal, a persecutor of the church; as to the righteousness which is in the Law, found blameless.

"But whatever things were gain to me, these things I have counted as loss because of Christ. More than that, I count all things to be loss in view of the surpassing value of knowing Christ Jesus my Lord, for whom I have suffered the loss of all things, and count them mere rubbish, so that I may gain Christ, and may be found in Him, not having a righteousness of my own derived from the Law, but that which is through faith in Christ, the righteousness which comes from God on the basis of faith, that I may know Him and the power of His resurrection and the fellowship of His sufferings, being conformed to His death; if somehow I may attain to the resurrection from the dead.

"Not that I have already grasped it all or have already become perfect, but I press on if I may also take hold of that for which I was even taken hold of by Christ Jesus. Brothers and sisters, I do not regard myself as having taken hold of it yet; but one thing I do: forgetting what lies behind and reaching forward to what lies ahead, I press on toward the goal for the prize of the upward call of God in Christ Jesus. Therefore, all who are mature, let's have this attitude; and if in anything you have a different attitude, God will reveal that to you as well; however, let's keep living by that same standard to which we have attained.

"Brothers and sisters, join in following my example, and observe those who walk according to the pattern you have in us. For many walk, of whom I often told you, and now tell you even as I weep, that they are the enemies of the cross of Christ, whose end is destruction, whose god is their appetite, and whose glory is in their shame, who have their minds on earthly things. For our citizenship is in heaven, from which we also eagerly wait for a Savior, the Lord Jesus Christ; who will transform the body of our lowly condition into conformity with His glorious body, by the exertion of the power that He has even to subject all things to Himself" (Philippians 3:3-21).

Paul continues, "We have this kind of confidence toward God through Christ. It is not that we are competent in ourselves to consider anything as coming from ourselves, but our competence is from God.

"Whenever a person turns to the Lord, the veil is removed. Now the Lord is the Spirit, and where the Spirit of the Lord is, there is freedom. We all, with unveiled faces, are looking as in a mirror at the glory of the Lord and are being transformed into the same image from glory to glory; this is from the Lord who is the Spirit" (2 Corinthians 3:4-5, 16-18).

When we stand before the judgment seat of Christ, the ones that will be found worthy of the kingdom of heaven are those that have done the will of God. They are the ones that have submitted totally to the Lordship of Jesus in their lives. They are the ones that humbled themselves and allowed the Holy Spirit to do His sanctifying work in their hearts. They are the ones that by the power of God working within them have been transformed and were conformed to the image of Christ. This transformation is from the Lord who is the Spirit.

Don't be deceived! When Paul writes in 1 Corinthians 15:51-52, "We will all be changed, in a moment, in the twinkling of an eye, at the last trumpet," he is not talking about our soul being conformed to the image of Christ. He is speaking of our body being changed from the natural body to the spiritual body.

This is clearly explained in the preceding verses. "So also is the resurrection of the dead. The body is sown perishable; it is raised imperishable. It is sown in dishonor; it is raised in glory. It is sown in weakness; it is raised in power. It is sown a natural body; it is raised a spiritual body. There is a natural body and there is also a spiritual body.

"So also it is written, 'The first man, Adam, became a living soul.' The last Adam became a life-giving spirit. However that which is spiritual isn't first, but that which is natural, then that

Walking in the Light

which is spiritual. The first man is of the earth, made of dust. The second man is the Lord from heaven.

"As is the one made of dust, such are those who are also made of dust; and as is the heavenly, such are they also that are heavenly. As we have borne the image of those made of dust, let's also bear the image of the heavenly. Now I say this, brothers, that flesh and blood can't inherit God's Kingdom; neither does the perishable inherit imperishable.

"Behold, I tell you a mystery. We will not all sleep, but we will all be changed, in a moment, in the twinkling of an eye, at the last trumpet. For the trumpet will sound and the dead will be raised incorruptible, and we will be changed."

The transformation of the soul must happen now, in this life. If we wait until we meet the Lord, it will be too late. Our destiny will already have been sealed. Don't be fooled. You cannot live for the flesh now and expect that the Lord will make everything okay when you meet Him. I'm sorry, but it doesn't work that way. We will reap what we sow.

Paul warns us, "Don't be deceived. God is not mocked, for whatever a man sows, that he will also reap. For he who sows to his own flesh will from the flesh reap corruption. But he who sows to the Spirit will from the Spirit reap eternal life" (Galatians 6:7-8).

Peter encourages us, revealing the goal of our faith, saying, "You love Him, though you have not seen Him. And though not seeing Him now, you believe in Him and rejoice with inexpressible and glorious joy, because you are receiving the goal of your faith, the salvation of your souls" (1 Peter 1:7-8, HCSB).

Now, in this age, we are receiving the goal of our faith, the salvation of our souls. Today is the day of salvation. This salvation of our souls, this being conformed to the image of Christ, is not something that will happen in the next age. It must take place now, between the time we are born again until we go to meet the Lord.

Peter continues to exhort us saying, "Therefore prepare your minds for action. Be sober, and set your hope fully on the grace that will be brought to you at the revelation of Jesus Christ— as children of obedience, not conforming yourselves according to your former lusts as in your ignorance, but just as he who called you is holy, you yourselves also be holy in all of your behavior; because it is written, 'You shall be holy; for I am holy.'

"If you call on him as Father, who without respect of persons judges according to each man's work, pass the time of your living as foreigners here in reverent fear . . . Seeing you have purified your souls in your obedience to the truth through the Spirit in sincere brotherly affection, love one another from the heart fervently, having been born again, not of corruptible seed, but of incorruptible, through the word of God, which lives and remains forever" (1 Peter 1:13-17, 22-23).

Those that will be found worthy of the kingdom of heaven will be those that have gained Christ in this life. They will be the ones that will be found in Him, not having a righteousness of their own, but that which is through faith in Christ, the righteousness from God based on faith. They will be the ones that know Him and the power of His resurrection and the fellowship of His sufferings and have been conformed unto His death.

They will be the ones that were careful about how they walked, realizing that the time is short. They will be the ones that walk, not as unwise, but as wise, making the most of the time, because the days are evil. They will not be foolish. They will understand what the Lord's will is and they will live according to it, that they might be pleasing to Him in all things.

How is it with you? Are you living a life that is pleasing to God in all things? Does your life honor Him in all you do and say?

"God now commands all people everywhere to repent, because He has set a day when He is going to judge the world in righteousness by the Man He has appointed. He has provided proof of this to everyone by raising Him from the dead" (Acts 17:30-31).

Walking in the Light

Remember, it is never too late to repent and turn back to God. Jesus is still calling to the weary, heavily burdened sinners to come to Him that they might find rest for their souls.

How is it with your soul?

Chapter 15 Discussion Questions:
Worthy of the Kingdom

1. Will every professing Christian be allowed to enter into the kingdom of heaven?
2. What did Jesus say to the professing Christians that did not do the will of His Father in heaven?
3. Will those who practice the works of the flesh inherit God's kingdom?
4. What is the Spirit warring against?
5. Why was the apostle John writing to the believers in 1John 2:1-6?
6. How can we know that we have come to know Jesus?
7. How should the one who says he remains in Christ walk?
8. If anyone loves the world, what is not in him?
9. His divine power gives us everything required for what?
10. Why are we easily deceived?
11. Who is of the Devil?
12. Who remains in Christ?
13. Who have no confidence in the flesh?
14. Who will be found worthy of the kingdom of heaven.
15. What can not inherit God's kingdom?
16. When must the transformation of the soul take place?
17. What is the goal of our faith?

Chapter 16

An Intimate Relationship

"In the beginning was the Word, and the Word was with God, and the Word was God. The same was in the beginning with God. All things were made through him. Without him, nothing was made that has been made. In him was life, and the life was the light of men" (John 1:1-4).

When God the Father set His mind to create the universe and all that it entails, He spoke the Word. The Word that was with God the Father came forth from Him. It was by the power of the Word that all things were made.

In the Word was life, and that life was the light of men. When God commanded the light to shine in Genesis 1:3, the whole of creation began to declare the glory and the promise of God in the Word. This light brought knowledge of God's purpose, giving meaning to all of creation.

Paul explains, "What can be known about God is evident among them (the people), because God has shown it to them. For His invisible attributes, that is, His eternal power and divine nature, have been clearly seen since the creation of the world, being understood through what He has made. As a result, people are without excuse" (Romans 1:20-21, HCSB).

John presents this wonderful truth, "For God so loved the world, that he gave his one and only Son, that whoever believes in him should not perish, but have eternal life" (John 3:16). The Word of God came forth from the Father and therefore is known as the Son of God.

By coming forth from the Father as the only Son, a very special intimate relationship was formed. We get a brief glimpse of the significance of this relationship in Proverbs 17:6. "The glory of sons is their fathers." Jesus prayed, "And now You, Father, glorify Me together with Yourself, with the glory which I had with You before the world existed" (John 17:5).

The writer of Hebrews tells us, "The Son is the radiance of God's glory and the exact representation of his being, sustaining all things by his powerful word" (Hebrews 1:3). The Word is so incredibly powerful that He not only created all things, but by His power all things are maintained and continue to exist. He upholds all things by the power of His hand. The scriptures declare, "He is before all things, and in him all things are held together" (Colossians 1:17).

The Word, who possessed all the power, all the wisdom, all of the attributes of divinity, voluntarily emptied Himself of everything divine and assumed the form of a slave and took on the likeness of a man. Paul writes about the Word saying, "Christ Jesus, who, existing in the form of God, did not consider equality with God as something to be used for His own advantage. Instead He emptied Himself by assuming the form of a slave, taking on the likeness of men" (Philippians 2:6-7).

According to John, "The Word became flesh and lived among us. We saw his glory, such glory as of the one and only Son of the Father, full of grace and truth" (John 1:14). The Word took on the likeness of man, being born, in the flesh, as a baby. That baby was given the name 'Jesus'. He was born, becoming flesh, as the result of the Holy Spirit of God impregnating the virgin, Mary (Luke 1:26-38).

When Jesus became flesh, born of the virgin, He became the first born of many brothers. Paul writes to the believers in Rome referring to Jesus saying, "He would be the firstborn among many brothers" (Romans 8:29, HCSB). Who are these many bothers that Jesus, the only Son of the Father, would become the first born of?

Jesus reveals the answer to this question in Matthew 12:50 saying, "For whoever does the will of my Father who is in heaven, he is my brother, and sister, and mother." Jesus explains further saying, "Not everyone who says to me, 'Lord, Lord,' will enter into the Kingdom of Heaven, but he who does the will of my Father who is in heaven" (Matthew 7:21).

Jesus discloses that only those that have been born physically as flesh and blood, born of water, and have been born spiritually, born of the Spirit are able to enter the kingdom of heaven. Jesus continued to explain saying, "Most certainly I tell you, unless one is born of water and spirit, he can't enter into God's Kingdom. That which is born of the flesh is flesh. That which is born of the Spirit is spirit" (John 3:5-6).

As a baby, Jesus was born of the Spirit and of water, both at the same time. Therefore, He was, from birth, like His brothers in every way. He was the first born of many brothers, born of water and born of the Spirit.

Everyone living today has been born with a physical body, born of water. However, because of Adam's sin, their spirit is dead. They are all dead in their trespasses (Ephesians 2:5). This is why we must be born again. Our spirit must be made alive by the Holy Spirit. When this happens, by faith in Jesus, we become one of the many brothers of Jesus.

The writer of Hebrews explains, "For the One who sanctifies and those who are sanctified all have one Father. That is why Jesus is not ashamed to call them brothers... Now since the children have flesh and blood in common, Jesus also shared in these, so that through His death He might destroy the one holding the power of death—that is, the Devil— and free those who were held in slavery all their lives by the fear of death... Therefore, He had to be like His brothers in every way, so that He could become a merciful and faithful high priest in service to God, to make propitiation for the sins of the people. For since He Himself was tested and has suffered, He is able to help those who are tested" (Hebrews 2:11, 14-15, 17-18, HCSB).

Jesus emptied Himself of all His divine attributes, not seeing them as something to be used for His own advantage to ease and protect His life while here on earth. He took on the form of a slave. He had no beauty that we should desire Him (Isaiah 53:2).

Luke sets forth this account in his gospel, "When eight days were fulfilled for the circumcision of the child, his name was called Jesus, which was given by the angel before he was conceived in the womb. When the days of their purification according to the law of Moses were fulfilled, they (His earthly parents) brought him up to Jerusalem, to present him to the Lord" (Luke 2:21-22).

"When they had accomplished all things that were according to the law of the Lord, they returned into Galilee, to their own city, Nazareth. The child was growing, and was becoming strong in spirit, being filled with wisdom, and the grace of God was upon him" (Luke 2:39-40). "And Jesus increased in wisdom and stature, and in favor with God and men" (Luke 2:52).

"Now when all the people were baptized, Jesus also had been baptized, and was praying. The sky was opened, and the Holy Spirit descended in a bodily form like a dove on him; and a voice came out of the sky, saying 'You are my beloved Son. In you I am well pleased.' Jesus himself, when he began to teach, was about thirty years old" (Luke 3:21-23). This was the beginning of the public portion of His earthly ministry.

"Jesus, full of the Holy Spirit, returned from the Jordan, and was led by the Spirit into the wilderness for forty days, being tempted by the devil. He ate nothing in those days. Afterward, when they were completed, he was hungry.

The devil said to him, 'If you are the Son of God, command this stone to become bread.' Jesus answered him, saying, 'It is written, 'Man shall not live by bread alone, but by every word of God'" (Luke 4:1-4).

"When the devil had completed every temptation, he departed from him until another time. Jesus returned in the power of the Spirit into Galilee, and news about him spread through all the surrounding area" (Luke 4:13-14).

"He came to Nazareth, where he had been brought up. He entered, as was his custom, into the synagogue on the Sabbath day, and stood up to read. The book of the prophet Isaiah was handed to him. He opened the book, and found the place where it was written, 'The Spirit of the Lord is on me, because he has anointed me to preach good news to the poor. He has sent me to heal the broken hearted, to proclaim release to the captives, recovering of sight to the blind, to deliver those who are crushed, and to proclaim the acceptable year of the Lord.'

"He closed the book, gave it back to the attendant, and sat down. The eyes of all in the synagogue were fastened on him. He began to tell them, 'Today, this Scripture has been fulfilled in your hearing'" (Luke 4:16-21).

The Word had emptied Himself of all His Godly powers and became a man of flesh and blood. Being born of the Spirit, He was born with a spirit that was alive and enabled Him to have fellowship with His heavenly Father. He could continually commune with the Father, praying always.

Yet, He still found it necessary to go apart from the noise and the busyness of the world and His ministry to spend time alone with the Father. Sometimes He would withdraw and spend all night in prayer, listening to and learning from the Father.

Walking in obedience to all that the Father had shown Him in these times of prayer, Jesus went forth into the world proclaiming the good news of the kingdom of God, casting out demons, and healing the sick. He began to preach, "Repent! For the Kingdom of Heaven is at hand" (Matthew 4:17). As He continued to walk in obedience, He called a few men to follow Him and they became His disciples.

After Jesus had spent much time with His disciples demonstrating to them His walk of faith in total submission to the Father, He sent them out in pairs and gave them authority over unclean spirits. His disciples went out and preached that people should repent. They drove out many demons and anointed many of the sick, healing them.

Walking in the Light

As soon as His disciples returned to Him and reported all that they had done, Jesus said to them, "'Come apart into a deserted place, and rest awhile.' For there were many coming and going, and they had no leisure so much as to eat. They went away in the boat to a deserted place by themselves" (Mark 6:31-32).

News came to Jesus about John the Baptist being beheaded while in prison. "Now when Jesus heard this, he withdrew from there in a boat to a deserted place apart" (Matthew 14:13). As Jesus returned to shore, He saw a large crowd gathered. He felt compassion for them and healed their sick.

When evening came the crowds became hungry. Jesus took the five loaves and two fish, and looking up to heaven He blessed them and broke them and gave them to the disciples to give to the crowd. After everyone ate and were filled, they picked up twelve baskets full of pieces left over. Immediately after the feeding of the 5,000, when Jesus had sent the multitudes away, "he went up into the mountain by himself to pray. When evening had come, he was there alone" (Matthew 14:23).

Jesus had such a close intimate relationship with His Father, that He was totally dependent on Him for everything. Apart from His Father, Jesus could do nothing. Jesus explains this to His disciples saying, "I can of mine own self do nothing: as I hear, I judge: and my judgment is just; because I seek not mine own will, but the will of the Father which hath sent me. . . The works which the Father hath given me to finish, the same works that I do, bear witness of me, that the Father hath sent me" (John 5:30, 36; KJV).

"Jesus said, 'When you have lifted up the Son of Man, then you will know that I am he and that I do nothing on my own but speak just what the Father has taught me'" (John 8:28, NIV). "If I don't do the works of my Father, don't believe me. But if I do them, though you don't believe me, believe the works, that you may know and believe that the Father is in me, and I in the Father" (John 10:37-38).

"For I spoke not from myself, but the Father who sent me, he gave me a commandment, what I should say, and what I should speak. I know that his commandment is eternal life. The things therefore which I speak, even as the Father has said to me, so I speak" (John 12:49-50).

"Don't you believe that I am in the Father, and the Father in me? The words that I tell you, I speak not from myself; but the Father who lives in me does his works. Believe me that I am in the Father, and the Father in me; or else believe me for the very works' sake" (John 14:10-11).

In His communion with the Father in prayer, Jesus would learn what the Father would want Him to do, and what the Father would want Him to say. Then He would do the works that the Father gave Him to do and He would speak the words the Father gave Him to speak. The indwelling Holy Spirit would enable Him to hear the Father and empower Him to obey the Father. His ministry was simply to do the will of the Father.

Jesus would pray to the Father according to the Father's will that had been shown to Him, and the Father would work the miracles according to what He had told Jesus He would do. As Jesus walked by faith, obeying all the Father had shown Him to do, the Father would do those works through Jesus. Thus it was the Father, by His divine power, doing His works through Jesus, and therefore all the works Jesus did were the works of the Father.

This faithfulness of Jesus, to do all that was shown to Him, is reminiscent of Moses doing all that God had shown Him. "Moses did everything just as the LORD commanded him" (Exodus 40:16, NIV).

According to Hebrews, "Moses indeed was faithful in all his house as a servant, for a testimony of those things which were afterward to be spoken, but Christ is faithful as a Son over his house. We are his house, if we hold fast our confidence and the glorying of our hope firm to the end" (Hebrews 3:5-6).

Walking in the Light

This relationship between Jesus, the Son, and God, the Father, is the most intimate relationship any human being could ever experience. The Son trusting the Father, for His faithful love and full provision of direction and guidance in every situation, even to the point of laying down His life according to the Father's will. The Father trusting the Son, to deny Himself completely, enduring to the end, throughout the incredible humiliation and suffering He experienced during His life and especially in His crucifixion and death.

Their trust was a reflection of the relationship they shared before the world began. It was a reflection of the glory they shared before the world even existed. Their relationship was so close, so intimate, that they were truly one, the Father in the Son and the Son in the Father.

I do not believe there is any passage of scripture that more eloquently expresses the incredible intimacy that Jesus had with His Father than His prayer just before His arrest and crucifixion. He had resigned Himself to voluntarily lay down His life, that the will of His Father would be fully accomplished through Him.

Looking up to heaven, Jesus prayed, "Father, the hour has come; glorify Your Son, so that the Son may glorify You, just as You gave Him authority over all mankind, so that to all whom You have given Him, He may give eternal life. And this is eternal life, that they may know You, the only true God, and Jesus Christ whom You have sent. I glorified You on the earth by accomplishing the work which You have given Me to do. And now You, Father, glorify Me together with Yourself, with the glory which I had with You before the world existed.

"I have revealed Your name to the men whom You gave Me out of the world; they were Yours and You gave them to Me, and they have followed Your word. Now they have come to know that everything which You have given Me is from You; for the words which You gave Me I have given to them; and they received them and truly understood that I came forth from You, and they believed that You sent Me. I ask on their behalf; I do not ask on behalf of the world, but on the behalf of those whom You have given Me, because they are Yours; and all things that are Mine are Yours, and Yours are Mine; and I have been glorified in them. I am no longer going to be in the world; and yet they themselves are in the world, and I am coming to You.

"Holy Father, keep them in Your name, the name which You have given Me, so that they may be one just as We are. While I was with them, I was keeping them in Your name, which You have given Me; and I guarded them, and not one of them perished except the son of destruction, so that the Scripture would be fulfilled.

"But now I am coming to You; and these things I speak in the world so that they may have My joy made full in themselves. I have given them Your word; and the world has hated them because they are not of the world, just as I am not of the world. I am not asking You to take them out of the world, but to keep them away from the evil one. They are not of the world, just as I am not of the world.

"Sanctify them in the truth; Your word is truth. Just as You sent Me into the world, I also sent them into the world. And for their sakes I sanctify Myself, so that they themselves also may be sanctified in truth.

"I am not asking on behalf of these alone, but also for those who believe in Me through their word, that they may all be one; just as You, Father, are in Me and I in You, that they also may be in Us, so that the world may believe that You sent Me.

"The glory which You have given Me I also have given to them, so that they may be one, just as We are one; I in them and You in Me, that they may be perfected in unity, so that the world may know that You sent Me, and You loved them, just as You loved Me. Father, I desire that they also, whom You have given Me, be with Me where I am, so that they may see My glory which You have given Me, for You loved Me before the foundation of the world.

"Righteous Father, although the world has not known You, yet I have known You; and these have known that You sent Me; and I have made Your name known to them, and will make it known, so that the love with which You loved Me may be in them, and I in them" (John 17:1-26, NASB).

Jesus, fully aware of the wondrous nature of His intimate relationship with His heavenly Father, prayed in verse 11, that His disciples would experience this same intimacy. "Holy Father, keep them through your name which you have given me, that they may be one, even as we are."

Christ died and rose again that we might experience the same intimacy as He had with the Father. Christ endured to the end, empowered by the Holy Spirit to both know and to do the Father's will.

He did this that we might now freely partake of this same oneness that He had with the Father, the most intimate relationship possible for any human being to experience. Praise the Lord, this intimate relationship is now freely available, by faith, to every person in Christ!

Chapter 16 Discussion Questions:
An Intimate Relationship

1. Through whom were all things created?
2. Why are people without excuse?
3. Why is the Word of God known as the Son of God?
4. Who is the exact representation of God the Father?
5. What did the Jesus empty Himself of to become like His brothers in every way?
6. What did the man Jesus have in common with His brothers?
7. Why is Jesus not ashamed to call us His brothers?
8. Why is Jesus able to help those who are tested?
9. Why would Jesus go apart to pray?
10. What did Jesus do on His own?
11. How did Jesus know what works He was to do and what words He was to speak?
12. What was Jesus' ministry?

13. What is the most intimate relationship any human being can experience?
14. What passage in scripture most eloquently expresses the intimacy that Jesus had with His Father?
15. In His prayer in John 17, what does Jesus ask of the Father for those that would believe in Him?
16. To whom is this intimate relationship now available?

Chapter 17

Following in His Steps

As we saw in the previous chapter, "Christ Jesus, who, existing in the form of God, did not consider equality with God as something to be used for His own advantage. Instead He emptied Himself by assuming the form of a slave, taking on the likeness of men. And when He had come as a man in His external form, He humbled Himself by becoming obedient to the point of death — even to death on a cross (Philippians 2:5-13, HCSB).

The writer of the book of Hebrews, directed by the Holy Spirit, speaks about Jesus and His brothers, the born-again Christians, saying, "For both He (Jesus) who sanctifies and those who are sanctified are all from one Father; for this reason He is not ashamed to call them brothers. . . Since the children share in flesh and blood, He Himself (Jesus) likewise also partook of the same, so that through death He might destroy the one who has the power of death, that is, the devil, and free those who through fear of death were subject to slavery all their lives.

"Therefore, in all things He (Jesus) had to be made like His brothers so that He might become a merciful and faithful high priest in things pertaining to God, to make propitiation for the sins of the people. For since He Himself was tempted in that which He has suffered, He is able to come to the aid of those who are tempted" (Hebrews 2:11, 14-15, 17-18, NASB).

The prophet Isaiah wrote about Jesus, the coming Messiah, saying, "He has no good looks or majesty. When we see him, there is no beauty that we should desire him. He was despised and rejected by men, a man of suffering and acquainted with disease. He was despised as one from whom men hide their face; and we didn't respect him" (Isaiah 53:2-3).

Jesus wasn't some invincible superhero or some glamourous movie idol or popstar. He didn't win any popularity contest. He was just like us. He was just like His brothers.

In fact, Jesus was like His brothers in every respect. Both He and His brothers were flesh and blood, without any supernatural powers of divinity. Both He and His brothers were tempted through the things that they suffered. Both He and His brothers had the same spiritual Father, God Himself in heaven. Both He and His brothers had spirits that had been made alive by being born from above, born of the Spirit (John 3:6). Jesus and His brothers were the same in every way.

In the previous chapter, we saw in detail the practical outworking of the incredibly intimate relationship that Jesus, the Son, had with God, the Father. We saw how Jesus was completely dependent on the Father, how He did nothing of Himself, but what the Father had shown Him.

We saw how He, in His total dependence on the Father, spent much time in prayer, not just casting all His cares upon the Father, but also listening and learning of the Father's will. There were many occasions when He would withdraw from the busyness of life to be alone with the Father, spending long periods of time being refreshed and strengthened in the Father's presence.

Here is a real test of whether we believe the scriptures. The scriptures say that upon being born again, upon becoming a brother in Christ, we are the same, in every respect, as Jesus was when He walked on this earth as a man. When we are baptized by the Holy Spirit into Christ, we become a new creation. We become brothers of Christ and sons of the Father.

As sons, we can have that same intimate relationship with the Father, right now, in the midst of this wicked perverse generation. As sons, we are like Jesus in every respect. We are flesh and blood, but now, with our spirit having been made alive by the Spirit of Christ indwelling our spirit, we can have an intimate relationship with the Father. We can commune with the Father, praying always (1 Thessalonians 5:17).

Being made to be exactly the same as Jesus was while He was in this world, the Father expects the same relationship with us as He had with Jesus. The Father expects us to be totally dependent on Him as He enables us and empowers us in the exact same way that He did with Jesus, through the indwelling Holy Spirit, to have this intimate relationship with Himself.

When we commune with the Father in prayer, He speaks to us by His Spirit, revealing His will to us, just as He did with Jesus. Sometimes it is necessary, because of the cares of our lives, to come apart from all the noise and busyness of the world and spend time alone with the Father.

When we spend time with the Father in prayer, we not only make requests by casting all of our cares upon Him, but more importantly, we listen to Him as He, by His Spirit, speaks to us. As He speaks to us, He reveals His will to us. He shows us what He wants us to say and what He wants us to do.

As we see the works the Father is doing and hear the words that He is speaking, our ministry is simply to obey Him as He enables us to hear and empowers us to do His will. We do this by praying to Him, asking Him that His will would be done, and trusting Him to do it. He then accomplishes His will, doing His works and speaking His words, through us and through others.

After His death, burial, and resurrection, Jesus spent 40 days proving to His disciples that He was indeed alive. During this time, Jesus commanded His disciples, 'Don't depart from Jerusalem, but wait for the promise of the Father, which you heard from me. For John indeed baptized in water, but you will be baptized in the Holy Spirit not many days from now. . . You will receive power when the Holy Spirit has come upon you. You will be witnesses to me in Jerusalem, in all Judea and Samaria, and to the uttermost parts of the earth'" (Acts 1:4-5, 8).

Jon von Ernst

Upon being baptized by the Holy Spirit, the disciples were immediately empowered by the Spirit to declare the magnificent acts of God. Being empowered by the Spirit, Peter rose up and spoke to the crowd that had gathered around them saying, "'This Jesus God raised up, to which we all are witnesses. Being therefore exalted by the right hand of God, and having received from the Father the promise of the Holy Spirit, he has poured out this, which you now see and hear. . . Let all the house of Israel therefore know certainly that God has made him both Lord and Christ, this Jesus whom you crucified.'

"Now when they heard this, they were cut to the heart, and said to Peter and the rest of the apostles, 'Brothers, what shall we do?'

"Peter said to them, 'Repent, and be baptized, every one of you, in the name of Jesus Christ for the forgiveness of sins, and you will receive the gift of the Holy Spirit. For the promise is to you, and to your children, and to all who are far off, even as many as the Lord our God will call to himself.' With many other words he testified, and exhorted them, saying, 'Save yourselves from this crooked generation!'

"Then those who gladly received his word were baptized. There were added that day about three thousand souls. They continued steadfastly in the apostles' teaching and fellowship, in the breaking of bread, and prayer" (Acts 2:32-33, 36-42).

Before being baptized by the Holy Spirit into Christ, the disciples were selfish and fearful. Immediately upon being baptized by the Holy Spirit, they became new creations (2 Corinthians 5:17). Immediately they were changed from being selfish and fearful, into being selfless and bold. After being born-again, baptized by the Spirit into Christ, they rejoiced in being counted worthy to suffer for the name of Jesus and for the gospel of the kingdom (Acts 5:41).

Before being baptized by the Spirit, their minds were concerned about the things of man (Matthew 16:21-23). After being baptized by the Spirit, their minds were set on the things

Walking in the Light

of the Spirit, understanding the will of the Father (Romans 12:1-2).

This is the experience of everyone that is baptized by the Spirit into Christ. Everyone born of the Spirit becomes a new creation when the Holy Spirit enters into their spirit to make it alive and to abide there with them (John 3:6).

In order to be like Jesus in every respect, we must be born again, we must have the Holy Spirit living, abiding in our spirit. Unfortunately, many professing Christians have never been born again, they have never received the Holy Spirit.

If you are one that has never received the Holy Spirit, you may be asking, "How can I receive the Holy Spirit? What do I need to do?"

Do not despair. Our heavenly Father wants to give us the Holy Spirit. All He requires is that we, believing in the Lord Jesus Christ, ask Him. It is that simple (Luke 11:9-13).

I believe that many people never received the Spirit when they believed because they never even heard that there is a Holy Spirit. They had merely heard the gospel of repentance.

They may have been led to feel sorry for their sins. They may have been baptized in water. They may have even gone through the motions of repeating a prayer asking for forgiveness. But through this entire process, they never even heard that there was a Holy Spirit.

Since believing, they may have joined a church. They may have begun reading the Bible. They may have made vows about living for the Lord and ceasing from sin.

Yet, instead of embarking on lives overflowing with love, joy, and peace, they have experienced lives of struggle and frustration. They continually try to be better. They try to please God. But they find they do not have the power or the ability to do it. They need the Holy Spirit!

Can someone be born again and not know it? Can someone's spirit be made alive by the Holy Spirit and not know it? Can someone become a new creation and not know it? Can someone be transferred from darkness to light and not know it?

If you have been born again, if the Holy Spirit has come to indwell you, you will know it. He makes all things new. He empowers you. He teaches you. He comforts you. He equips you to hear the Lord and to obey His voice.

He overflows in you with love for the brothers, with joy in the Lord, and with praise and worship of our Father in heaven. The Spirit will completely change your life.

If you are not living a victorious Christian life, if you did not receive the Holy Spirit when you believed, I encourage you to simply ask our Father who is in heaven and He will give the Holy Spirit to you. Be persistent, keep asking, keep seeking, keep knocking and the door will be opened to you.

The Father will give the Holy Spirit to those who ask Him. We have Jesus's assurance on this. If we truly believe Jesus, we will believe His promise regarding the Father's faithfulness to give us the Holy Spirit.

Remember, God wants the best for us. He wants us to know everything that is ours in Christ. It is for this reason that He wants to give us His Holy Spirit, that we might be enabled to live holy lives to His praise and to His glory.

Upon being born of the Spirit, we become a new creation. Upon being baptized by the Holy Spirit into Christ, we become like Jesus, enabled by the Spirit to hear the Father speaking to us and empowered by the indwelling Holy Spirit to do the will of the Father.

"For while we were yet weak, at the right time Christ died for the ungodly. . . God commends his own love toward us, in that while we were yet sinners, Christ died for us. Much more then, being now justified by his blood, we will be saved from God's wrath through him. For if while we were enemies, we were reconciled to God through the death of his Son, much more, being reconciled, we will be saved by his life" (Romans 5:6-10).

Now having been reconciled to God, much more, we are being saved by grace, through His life working powerfully within us. Paul writes, "For by grace you are being saved through faith" (Ephesians 2:8, TFLV). Through exercising our faith to believe in Jesus, we are now in the process of being saved by grace. God gives this grace to those that have merited it by exercising their faith to believe in Jesus.

When, by faith in Christ Jesus, we are born again, baptized in the Holy Spirit, we not only experience our sins being forgiven and ourselves being reconciled to God, we also begin to experience the 'much more' that God has provided for us in Christ Jesus our Lord. We begin the process of sanctification, the process of being saved by grace through the power of His life working within us to accomplish God's will within each of us.

This will begins to be accomplished in us as we enter into a relationship with the Father. This relationship with the Father creates within each believer an innate desire to please Him in all things.

In pursuing this desire, we begin to experience, more and more, God's incredible love for us. We find that the more we demonstrate our love for His Son, Jesus Christ our Lord, by submitting completely to His authority as Lord, and obeying Him, the more we come to experience and understand this amazing love that God has for us.

Jesus encourages us, "Therefore you now have sorrow, but I will see you again, and your heart will rejoice, and no one will take your joy away from you. In that day you will ask me no questions. Most certainly I tell you, whatever you may ask of the Father in my name, he will give it to you.

"Until now, you have asked nothing in my name. Ask, and you will receive, that your joy may be made full. I have spoken these things to you in figures of speech. But the time is coming when I will no more speak to you in figures of speech, but will tell you plainly about the Father.

"In that day you will ask in my name; and I don't say to you that I will pray to the Father for you, for the Father himself loves you, because you have loved me, and have believed that I came from God. I came from the Father, and have come into the world. Again, I leave the world, and go to the Father" (John 16:22-28).

The Father desires to have an intimate relationship with each of His sons. He desires to have the same relationship with each of His sons that He had with Jesus while He was physically living among us in His body of flesh and blood.

The Father loves us because we have loved His son Jesus and have believed that Jesus came from the Father. We demonstrate the reality of our love for Jesus by obeying Him, by keeping His commands. In John 14:15, Jesus told His disciples "If you love Me, you will keep My commandments." Our total submission to Jesus as Lord in all obedience is the proof of the reality of our love for Him.

Paul asks, "Should we continue in sin so that grace may multiply? Absolutely not! How can we who died to sin still live in it? Or are you unaware that all of us who were baptized into Christ Jesus were baptized into His death?

"Therefore we were buried with Him by baptism into death, in order that, just as Christ was raised from the dead by the glory of the Father, so we too may walk in a new way of life. For if we have been joined with Him in the likeness of His death, we will certainly also be in the likeness of His resurrection.

"For we know that our old self was crucified with Him in order that sin's dominion over the body may be abolished, so that we may no longer be enslaved to sin. . . So, you too consider yourselves dead to sin but alive to God in Christ Jesus." (Romans 6:1-6, 11; HCSB).

The indwelling Spirit of Christ sets us free from the condemnation of being enslaved to sin and empowers us to live godly lives, now, in the midst of this crooked and perverse generation. If we have the Spirit of Christ, we are without excuse when we sin because God has given us everything we require to live holy lives, fully pleasing to Him.

Peter reminds us, "For His divine power has granted to us everything pertaining to life and godliness, through the true knowledge of Him who called us by His own glory and excellence. Through these He has granted to us His precious and magnificent promises, so that by them you may

Walking in the Light

become partakers of the divine nature, having escaped the corruption that is in the world on account of lust" (2 Peter 1:3-4).

Jesus challenges us to believe saying, "Don't you believe that I am in the Father, and the Father in me? The words that I tell you, I speak not from myself; but the Father who lives in me does his works. Believe me that I am in the Father, and the Father in me; or else believe me for the very works' sake.

"Most certainly I tell you, he who believes in me, the works that I do, he will do also; and he will do greater works than these, because I am going to my Father. Whatever you will ask in my name, I will do it, that the Father may be glorified in the Son. If you will ask anything in my name, I will do it" (John 14:10-14).

This is a huge part of our doing the will of the Father, believing the scriptures, believing that Jesus has given us much more than just the forgiveness of sins, even more than being reconciled to God. He has given us His life, and by His life we are being saved by grace through faith. We need to believe the scriptures. We need to believe God's precious and magnificent promises.

We need to believe God for our sanctification just as we believed Him for our reconciliation. We need to believe that God is able to empower us, by His indwelling Holy Spirit, to live godly lives, to be holy as He is Holy, to walk as Jesus walked, now, in the midst of this wicked and perverse generation.

Peter commands us, "In your hearts revere Christ as Lord. Always be prepared to give an answer to everyone who asks you to give the reason for the hope that you have. But do this with gentleness and respect" (1 Peter 3:15, NIV).

Paul wrote to the believers in Colossians 1:27, "Christ in you, the hope of glory!" Our only hope of glory is to have Christ living as Lord within us. Without Christ, as the Holy Spirit, abiding in our spirit, we are without hope in this world.

Paul explained this, writing to the believers in Ephesus. He encouraged them saying, "Therefore remember that once you, the Gentiles in the flesh, who are called 'uncircumcision' by that which is called 'circumcision' (in the flesh, made by hands), that you were at that time separate from Christ, alienated from the commonwealth of Israel, and strangers from the covenants of the promise, having no hope and without God in the world.

"But now in Christ Jesus you who once were far off are made near in the blood of Christ. For he is our peace, who made both one, and broke down the middle wall of separation, having abolished in his flesh the hostility, the law of commandments contained in ordinances, that he might create in himself one new man of the two, making peace, and might reconcile them both in one body to God through the cross, having killed the hostility through it.

"He came and preached peace to you who were far off and to those who were near. For through him we both have our access in one Spirit to the Father.

"So then you are no longer strangers and foreigners, but you are fellow citizens with the saints and of the household of God, being built on the foundation of the apostles and prophets, Christ Jesus himself being the chief cornerstone; in whom the whole building, fitted together, grows into a holy temple in the Lord; in whom you also are built together for a habitation of God in the Spirit" (Ephesians 2:11-22).

Paul continues this thought in the next chapter. "I was made a servant according to the gift of that grace of God which was given me according to the working of his power.

"To me, the very least of all saints, was this grace given, to preach to the Gentiles the unsearchable riches of Christ, and to make all men see what is the administration of the mystery which for ages has been hidden in God, who created all things through Jesus Christ, to the intent that now through the assembly the manifold wisdom of God might be made known to the principalities and the powers in the heavenly places, according to the eternal purpose which he accomplished in Christ Jesus our Lord.' In him we have boldness and access in confidence through our faith in him. Therefore I ask that you may not lose heart at my troubles for you, which are your glory.

"For this cause, I bow my knees to the Father of our Lord Jesus Christ, from whom every family in heaven and on earth is named, that he would grant you, according to the riches of his glory, that you may be strengthened with power through his Spirit in the inner person, that Christ may dwell in your hearts through faith, to the end that you, being rooted and grounded in love, may be strengthened to comprehend with all the saints what is the width and length and height and depth, and to know Christ's love which surpasses knowledge, that you may be filled with all the fullness of God.

"Now to him who is able to do exceedingly abundantly above all that we ask or think, according to the power that works in us, to him be the glory in the assembly and in Christ Jesus to all generations forever and ever. Amen" (Ephesians 3:7-20).

Paul is explaining to the believers how God the Father works mightily within each believer according to the power of the Holy Spirit that works within them. It is this Spirit of Christ within the believer that brings the believer into that same intimate relationship that Jesus Himself experienced with the Father.

We are strengthened with the power of God through His Spirit in the inner man. Our old man, the outer man, the man controlled by the power of the sin in our flesh, was crucified with Christ. This death with Christ set us free from the condemnation of being enslaved to sin. Now we are being strengthened in the inner man by the empowering of the indwelling Spirit within our spirit.

Now, by the power of the indwelling Spirit of Christ working mightily according to His great strength, we are being conformed not to this world, but to the image of Christ. We are being transformed by the renewing of our minds.

Paul entreats us, "Therefore I urge you, brothers, by the mercies of God, to present your bodies a living sacrifice, holy, acceptable to God, which is your spiritual service. Don't be conformed to this world, but be transformed by the renewing of your mind, so that you may prove what is the good, well-pleasing, and perfect will of God" (Romans 12:1-2).

Jesus said, "I am the way, the truth, and the life. No one comes to the Father, except through me" (John 14:6). And again, as Paul wrote in the passage above, "For through him (Christ) we both have our access in one Spirit to the Father."

Jesus died and was raised again that we might have access to the Father in one Spirit. But not to just have access, but to have an intimate relationship with the Father as sons. Christ, our eldest brother, brings us into this relationship with the Father when we walk by faith believing God, believing what God has spoken in the scriptures.

When we walk by faith, as Jesus walked by faith, we enter into the same intimate relationship with the Father that Jesus had. We enter into the same ability to live a godly life in full obedience to the Father, doing His will, pleasing Him in all things.

If we have a heart of unbelief, hardened by the deceitfulness of sin, not believing God, not trusting God as one that is able to accomplish in us, now in this age, everything He has promised in His word, we will not be able to enter into the rest He has for us. If we have a heart of unbelief, we will fall short of entering into all that God has prepared for us.

The writer of Hebrews warns us, "Beware, brothers, lest perhaps there might be in any one of you an evil heart of unbelief, in falling away from the living God; but exhort one another day by day, so long as it is called 'today', lest any one of you be hardened by the deceitfulness of sin. For we have become partakers of Christ, if we hold the beginning of our confidence firm to the end, while it is said, 'Today if you will hear his voice, don't harden your hearts, as in the rebellion.'

"For who, when they heard, rebelled? Wasn't it all those who came out of Egypt led by Moses? With whom was he displeased forty years? Wasn't it with those who sinned, whose bodies fell in the wilderness? To whom did he swear that they wouldn't enter into his rest, but to those who were disobedient? We see that they weren't able to enter in because of unbelief.

"Let's fear therefore, lest perhaps anyone of you should seem to have come short of a promise of entering into his rest. For indeed we have had good news preached to us, even as they also did, but the word they heard didn't profit them, because it wasn't mixed with faith by those who heard. For we who have believed do enter into that rest."

"For if Joshua had given them rest, he would not have spoken afterward of another day. There remains therefore a Sabbath rest for the people of God. For he who has entered into his rest has himself also rested from his works, as God did from his.

"Let's therefore give diligence to enter into that rest, lest anyone fall after the same example of disobedience. For the word of God is living and active, and sharper than any two-edged sword, piercing even to the dividing of soul and spirit, of both joints and marrow, and is able to discern the thoughts and intentions of the heart. There is no creature that is hidden from his sight, but all things are naked and laid open before the eyes of him to whom we must give an account" (Hebrews 3:12-19, 4:1-3, 8-13).

The believers that have entered into this intimate relationship with the Father have entered into the Sabath rest that God has prepared for His people. These believers have ceased from their own works and are resting in the intimate relationship with the Father that Jesus provided for them through His blood and His Spirit.

Jesus, in His walk of faith, strengthened by the Spirit through this intimate relationship with the Father, has provided us with the perfect example of how we, as born-again believers, are to live. Peter reveals this perfect example to us.

"Slaves, in reverent fear of God submit yourselves to your masters, not only to those who are good and considerate, but also to those who are harsh. For it is commendable if someone bears up under the pain of unjust suffering because they are conscious of God. But how is it to your credit if you receive a beating for doing wrong and endure it? But if you suffer for doing good and you endure it, this is commendable before God. To this you were called, because Christ suffered for you, leaving you an example, that you should follow in his steps.

"'He committed no sin, and no deceit was found in his mouth.' When they hurled their insults at him, he did not retaliate; when he suffered, he made no threats. Instead, he entrusted himself to him who judges justly" (1 Peter 2:18-23, NIV).

Trusting in God's love and faithfulness, let us follow this perfect example that has been provided for us in Jesus Christ our Lord, entrusting ourselves to Him who judges righteously. Let us follow in His steps that we might rejoice at His return.

Chapter 17 Discussion Questions:
Following in His Steps

1. Why did Christ Jesus, who existing in the form of God, empty Himself?
2. Why did Jesus have to be made like His brothers in every respect?
3. What things did Jesus and His brothers have in common?
4. What is a real test of whether we believe the scriptures?
5. As born-again believers, what kind of a relationship can we have with the Father?
6. What effect did being baptized in the Spirit have on the disciples?
7. What does the 'much more' in Romans 5:10 refer to?
8. According to John 16, why does the Father love us?
9. Why should the born-again believer not continue in sin?
10. Why was our old self crucified with Christ?
11. What empowers the born-again believer to live a holy life?
12. What is a huge part of our doing the will of the Father?

13. What is our hope of glory?
14. According to Ephesians 3, what did Paul preach to the Gentiles?
15. How is our inner man strengthened?
16. How can we know the perfect will of God?
17. What can the deceitfulness of sin do to the born-again believer?
18. Who have entered into the Sabbath rest that God has prepared for His people?
19. How can we follow in the steps of Christ?

Epilogue

Paul wrote to the Thessalonian believers to reassure them that the Day of the Lord would not come except the apostasy come first (2 Thessalonians 2:3). The Greek word translated as apostasy has been translated in various versions of the Bible as a falling away, departing, turning away, rebellion, or revolt. The literal meaning of the Greek word is 'defection from the truth.'

This is interesting because it is not just desertion, but defection. Desertion is when someone deserts their post, they just leave, they want nothing more to do with what they were previously a part of. Defection is much more serious. Defection is when someone not only leaves the side they were on but goes over to join the other side.

When someone defects from the truth, they leave the truth and join the side of error, the side of falsehood, the side of lies. Defection from the truth and embracing the lies of false teaching is extremely serious.

Paul told the Thessalonians this defection would happen before the Day of the Lord, before the antichrist, the man of lawlessness would be revealed. So, what does this apostasy, this defection from the truth have to do with us?

Defection from the truth does not happen overnight, it takes time, it involves a long gradual process. It is not easy to convince someone to move from embracing the truth, to opposing the truth and embracing a lie, undermining the faith.

It begins with a very small deviation, a very small error. It begins with a very subtle, seemingly innocent deception. It can begin with subtly changing the meaning of a word.

It can begin with changing the meaning of grace from favor to unmerited favor, or mercy. Making that little change seems so harmless. It appears to be an innocent attempt to clarify the meaning of the word so that it can be more easily related to by

Walking in the Light

the hearers. However, let's consider the ramifications of confusing the meaning of grace with the meaning of mercy.

Throughout scripture, God's favor, God's grace, was bestowed upon those who merited it, those that listened to Him and obeyed Him, those who were righteous. God favors the humble, those contrite in spirit, those that tremble at His word, but He resists the proud, the arrogant, the unrighteous, the ones that practice evil.

However, God imprisoned all in disobedience that He might have mercy on all. God's mercy, made available through Christ's death and resurrection, is freely available to all who would accept it.

A pivotal doctrine in the theology of false teachers, the assurance of salvation, needed support because it conflicted with the scriptures. They taught that believers are saved by grace alone, through faith alone, in Christ alone, with no requirement for any action of obedience or change in lifestyle.

They taught that once you believed, there was nothing you could do to lose your salvation. They assured professing believers that they were saved, no matter what they would do, their salvation was assured. They did nothing to earn it, and they could do nothing to lose it.

However, the believer's lives did not match up with what scripture revealed as God's expectation for them. God expects believers to live holy lives, to walk in obedience to Him. However, their experience was one of a continual struggle with sin because they were merely natural men, devoid of the Spirit.

Some began to doubt their salvation. So the false teachers changed grace from merited favor to unmerited, and taught that all sins, past, present, and future, were forgiven upon being saved. Thereby believer's consciences could be assuaged from any guilt or condemnation.

They also taught that Romans 7 was Paul's testimony as a Christian, even though Paul said, in that passage, that he practiced evil. The professing Christians were relieved to learn that they were not so bad, because Paul had the same struggle with sin, yet received God's grace.

The idea of God's grace being free and unmerited meant professing Christians could rest in the promise of never losing their salvation, no matter how wretched and sinful their lives might be. They were taught the comforting message of "Peace, peace!" when there was no peace.

Now they could, by virtue of their defection from the truth, go merrily on their way down the broad road that leads to destruction. Because they did not love the truth, because they did not know the scriptures or the power of God, they were easily deceived.

"Is the apostasy already taking place?" When we see these and other false teachings so readily embraced by the professing Christians in so many churches today, one has to wonder, "Is this the defection from the truth that Paul stated would take place before the Lord's return?"

Paul writes in 2 Thessalonians 2:10, "They perish because they did not accept the love of the truth in order to be saved." We must be those that have the love of the truth.

We must be those that are willing to go to the scriptures and allow the Spirit of Truth to teach us. We must allow God's word to shine its light into our hearts and expose any lie, any false teaching that we have received, embraced, and possibly even taught to others.

We must have such a love of the truth that we eagerly question everything we have been taught, everything we have come to believe, and examine each one in the light of the truth as revealed in the holy scriptures. We must learn to hate lies. We must learn to hate false teachings. This will only happen as we receive and accept from the Lord the love of the truth.

The deception of the coming days, the last days before the Lord's return, will be so great that, if possible, even the elect would be led astray (Matthew 24:24-25).

We must pray that God would give us this love of the truth. Only the love of the truth will save us from the incredible deception of these last days that are quickly approaching!